TARTUFFE

Andrew Hilton & Dominic Power

after Molière

Revised Edition

stf | Shakespeare at the Tobacco Factory

First published March 2017 by Shakespeare at the Tobacco
Factory
This revised edition published October 2017
by **Favell & Marsden**
in association with Shakespeare at the Tobacco Factory

ISBN 978 1 5272 1136 0

Introduction

Jean Baptiste Poquelin (Molière) was born in Paris in 1622, the son of one of the royal court's *valets de chambre tapissiers,* responsible for the care of the King's furniture and upholstery. He was educated at the Jesuit Collège de Clermont where the education would have included performing scenes from Latin theatre and instruction in rhetoric.

As the eldest son of the family, his father intended he should follow in his own footsteps, but at the age of 21 Jean Baptiste determined to make a life in the theatre, an enthusiasm that had been innocently encouraged by his maternal grandfather's own passion for playgoing.

It was an extraordinary decision for a middle-class young man with good prospects. Theatre was perhaps even less respectable in seventeenth century Paris than it was in Shakespeare's London, and may not have thrived at all had it not been for the patronage of the King. The Paris church routinely excommunicated professional actors and was to prove utterly unforgiving to Molière at the end of his life.

But Jean Baptiste had fallen in love with the actress Madeleine Béjart (he later married her daughter – some say her sister – Armande). In 1643, with Madeleine and about a dozen others, he formed the 'Illustre Théâtre' – soon changing his name to 'Molière', possibly to spare his family embarrassment.

The project was financially disastrous, earning Molière some periods in prison for debt, and in 1645 he and the rump of the company left the capital to work in the provinces, where they remained for over a decade. Out of the Paris spotlight, Molière began to write. His success as a dramatist and the maturing skills of the ensemble encouraged them to try their luck once more in Paris. On October 24th 1658, a performance of *Le Docteur Amoureux* so impressed the King and Court that the company was granted use of one of Paris' best theatres and the title of the 'Troupe de Monsieur' ('Monsieur' being Louis XIV's brother, the duc d'Orléans).

In 1663 royal patronage saw Molière being granted a pension of 1,000 livres, and in the following year the King agreed to be godfather to his first child, Louis. In 1665 the company became the 'Troupe du Roi', and Molière's annual pension was raised to 6,000 livres.

On February 17th 1673, the exhausted Molière suffered a haemorrhage while playing the role of the hypochondriac Argan in Le Malade Imaginaire. He died later that night at his home on the Rue Richelieu. The local priests refused to take his confession and forbade his burial in holy ground. The King, however, interceded and under the cover of darkness he was buried in the Cemetery Saint Joseph. In 1817 his remains were transferred to a fine tomb in the Père Lachaise Cemetery.

Tartuffe, finally publicly performed and published in 1669, portrays a wealthy Parisian citizen, Orgon, being duped by a bogus religious zealot who has inveigled his way into the household as Orgon's personal 'directeur de conscience'. Tartuffe prays louder and longer than anyone else in the local church, wears a hair shirt, self-flagellates, requires a female servant to cover her breast with linen, and claims to give what little money he has to the poor. His real object is to acquire all Orgon's property by alienating him from his son Damis and marrying his daughter Mariane against her will.

Molière presented the play's first three acts before the King and six hundred guests as part of a royal festival, Plaisirs de L'Ile Enchantée, at Versailles on May 12th 1664 – the first recorded performance, though there may have been other private events before this, very probably including one for the King. Certainly the play's theme was already known in court and church circles because just over a month before the festival the Compagnie du Saint-Sacrement, a secret but powerful Catholic society of churchmen, courtiers and parliamentarians, had met to discuss how they might "procure the suppression of the evil play of Tartuffe". At this point it seems the play was entitled 'Tartuffe, or The Hypocrite', and the actor playing Tartuffe was costumed as a priest, or at least as a minor churchman.

Five days later, whatever his private feelings about the play, and under pressure from the Compagnie du Saint-Sacrement, the Archbishop of Paris and the Parliament, the King banned its public performance. A few weeks later, in a vicious attack, the curé of

Saint-Barthelemy – calling Molière "that demon clad in human flesh" – urged that he be burned at the stake to expiate his crime, a fate that had actually befallen a Parisian lawyer only two years earlier for writing verses found similarly abhorrent. It is unlikely that Molière was in such danger, as he continued to enjoy the protection of the King, whose published reasoning for banning the play excused the dramatist from any malevolent intent.

In his Preface to the published version Molière protested about how hard he had worked to make it clear that his Tartuffe was not a hypocritical churchman, but an out-and-out scoundrel. But the church's sensitivity was well-grounded; there had been at least one incident – in Caen in 1660 – where members of the Compagnie du Saint-Sacrement themselves had been accused of abusing their privileged access to private households – and numerous other examples of hypocrisy by churchmen, including by Charpy de Sainte-Croix and the Abbé Roquette, who Saint-Simon referred to a century later as the "great beast on whom Molière based his Tartuffe".

By 1667 Molière had completed the play and retitled it 'The Imposter' – a title that carries a rather different message from 'The Hypocrite'. He had also changed the name of its central character to 'Panulfe', and now costumed him not as a cleric, but as a fashionable man in 'a small hat, a great wig, a large collar, a sword, and lace on everything'. Believing he had met the King's concerns, Molière opened the play on August 5th, but on the following day, in the absence of the King who was with his army in Flanders, it was banned by order of Parliament; and on the 11th the Archbishop of Paris forbade all people in his diocese from performing the play, or reading or hearing it read, in public or in private, on pain of excommunication.

Molière had to wait until 1669, when it seems the power of the church – and the Compagnie du Saint-Sacrement – had waned, before the King finally granted him the right to produce the play in the public theatre, and to publish it 'avec privilege du Roy'. Now entitled Tartuffe ou L'Imposteur it opened at the Palais-Royal on February 5th 1669, was published on March 23rd, and contributed largely to the most profitable season for Molière's company in his lifetime. It has remained one of the most popular plays in the French classical repertoire.

Tartuffe in English

The play was first translated into English by the actor Matthew Medbourne for performance in London in 1670, only months after the public première in Paris. This was also the first English *adaptation* of the play to meet English social conditions. Medbourne reimagined Molière's Roman Catholic Tartuffe as a hypocritical Puritan – an easy and no doubt popular target in the anglo-catholic world of Charles II. He also developed a character to whom Molière gave no words – and possibly not even an appearance – Tartuffe's servant, Laurent. Medbourne's Laurent falls in love with the maid Dorine and becomes the agency by which the family's fortunes are saved at the dénouement; the published text declares it "render'd into English with much addition and advantage by M. Medbourne".

The play was then plundered by the London theatre for both themes and devices, including in a 1689 play by John Crowne which – in a reversal of Medbourne's purpose – targeted the allegedly fraudulent behaviour of the Roman Catholic priesthood and their lay sympathisers.

There were later translations, including ones by Martin Clare in 1726 and Isaac Bickerstaffe in 1769, and in 1851 a successful production at the Haymarket, featuring the actor-manager Ben Webster as Tartuffe, in a text that claimed to be the first authentic rendering into English of Molière's 1669 version. During these decades there were also relatively frequent performances in London by visiting French companies.

Nonetheless, a translator of the play in 1898, Thomas Constable, mourned a general lack of enthusiasm for French classical theatre, writing in his Preface: "It is little to say that the masterpieces of the greatest French dramatists are not acted in England; except in schools they are hardly read."

Change did come to some degree after the 2nd World War, when the Comédie-Française performed *Tartuffe* in London in 1945 and again in 1951; and the Bristol Old Vic then pursued this renewed interest with a series of Molière plays in versions by Miles Malleson – including a *Tartuffe* in 1950.

Malleson's prose translations have been followed more recently by verse translations by Richard Wilbur (first produced in the U.K by the National Theatre in 1967); by Christopher Hampton (RSC at the Barbican 1983), Ranjit Bolt (NT 2002), and Roger McGough (Liverpool Playhouse 2008); with versions in Scots dialect by Liz Lochhead (Edinburgh Lyceum 1986) and an Asian version by Tara Arts (NT 1990).

In the U.S. there was an adaptation by Simon Gray at the Kennedy Centre in 1982, and a 'televangelist' version by Freyda Thomas – *Tartuffe: Born Again* – at the Circle in the Square in Washington in 1996.

Reinventing the play for 2017

Tartuffe has fascinated the theatre world, in France and elsewhere, for three and a half centuries, and its portrayal of a pillar of the community being captivated – against all logic and expectation – by a brazen impostor has now acquired an extra resonance.

So, from an initial idea some years ago to attempt a new translation of Molière's play, grew this bolder notion to reinvent the play for 2017.

Even so, we set out to follow Molière's pattern closely, speech by speech, and to write in rhyming couplets – not in Molière's 12 syllable-line Alexandrines, but in the 10 syllable pentameter line more familiar to the English ear. Both intentions became modified as we worked; while retaining the scene structure, we came to see no virtue in sticking to the speech template; and the end-stopped couplet became rarer and rarer, with great use of 'enjambement' (the sense flowing on beyond the rhyme into the next line), while internal rhyming even allowed us to break the couplet pattern altogether a number of times. In the end ear and instinct became our main referees.

Molière's Tartuffe wears a mask of Catholic zealotry and, in this, he is a man for Molière's time. He is also an enigma; we, and most members of the family he invades, recognise his hypocrisy, his lechery and his greed from the start, yet we do not know where he comes from or what causes him to be as he is. In our new era of alternative facts, fake news and political uncertainty, Tartuffe would surely find new opportunities for his guile. The mask he presents to his victims may have changed, but the self-invention, the opportunism and the appetites are timeless.

Between 1664 and 2017 there have, of course, been seismic changes in attitudes and family dynamics and we have adapted accordingly, while remaining essentially true to Molière's narrative. In one instance we have taken a greater liberty; Molière's *deus ex machina* is the offstage intervention of King Louis XIV. Since an intervention by our own royal family is even less probable, we indulge in a mild act of *lèse majesté* by providing our own catalyst for Act 5.

Andrew Hilton & Dominic Power

This version of Molière's *Tartuffe* was first presented by *Shakespeare at the Tobacco Factory* and *Tobacco Factory Theatres* on April 6th 2017 at the Tobacco Factory, Bristol, with the following cast:

DAME PAMELA OGDEN	Tina Gray
CHARLES OGDEN, her son, a Tory Junior Minister	Christopher Bianchi
EMMA LAWRENCE, her daughter-in-law	Saskia Portway
MELISSA OGDEN, Charles' daughter by his first wife	Daisy May
DANIEL OGDEN, Melissa's twin	Joel Macey
CLEM LAWRENCE, Emma's brother, a journalist	Philip Buck
DANUTA, the Ogdens' Polish live-in housekeeper	Anna Elijasz
VAL, a trainee lawyer, engaged to Melissa	Kenton Thomas
TARTUFFE, author of *Our Kid*	Mark Meadows
DES LOYAL, senior *Sunday Shocker* hack	Alan Coveney

Director	Andrew Hilton
Associate Director	Dominic Power
Assistant Director (Attachment)	Phoebe Simmonds
Set & Costume Designer	Sarah Warren
Costume Supervisor	Jane Tooze
Composer & Sound Designer	John Telfer
Lighting Designer	Matthew Graham
Production Photographer	Craig Fuller
Legal Adviser	Martin Davey

Producer	Morag Massey
Production Manager	Nic Prior
Construction Manager	Chris Samuels
Company & Stage Manager	Kevin Smith
Deputy Stage Manager	Samantha Mallinson
Assistant Stage Manager	Megan Hastings
Stage Management Support & Cover	Cassie Harrison
Wardrobe Mistress	Francine Gyll

A large reception room in a three-storey house in Hampstead Garden Suburb in North West London. There are doors to the hall and to the kitchen, and French windows to the garden. For three generations the house has been the London base for a busy family with more important things on their mind than domestic style, and their home has never been blessed by a thoroughgoing makeover. Charles Ogden's second wife, Emma, is content that she has room for her modern Yamaha piano, and the worn, green leather Chesterfield chimes happily with Charles' three decades on the Commons benches in Westminster.

Copies of Tartuffe's autobiography 'Our Kid' and the most recent edition of 'Wisden' are in evidence, as are a part-drunk bottle of Glen Ord whisky and some glasses.

Following Molière's Classical Theatre practice, the action takes place in this one location and on a single day – a high summer day – in the present.

Act One	10.00 am
Act Two	11.30 am
Act Three	12.30 pm
Interval	
Act Four	6.00 pm
Act Five	8.00 pm

A forward slash (/) indicates where the following speech should intervene

The text reflects U.K. politics as they stood in March 2017, with Theresa May heading a majority Conservative administration and Jeremy Corbyn leading the Labour Opposition. There are interesting possibilities of adaptation to meet changed circumstances – minority governments, coalitions or a Labour majority. But whichever pertains, junior Minister or only 'shadow', Charles Ogden remains (in Tartuffe's words) 'an old-school Tory'.

ACT ONE   10.00 am

As the audience enters, the piano is covered with a protective cloth

When the lights build on a sunny summer morning, CLEM is working on a MacBook, a pile of newspapers beside him, and the piano cloth is lying on the floor

DANIEL & MELISSA are at the piano, improvising a duet ...

THE MORAL ASCENDANCY BLUES

DANIEL	*Well, I've been down but now I'm up,*
BOTH	*Well, I've been down but now I'm up,*
MELISSA	*Well I been poor but now my cup runneth over. I'm always moral,*
DANIEL	*Get what I want without a quarrel, just walk and talk and preach like Jesus,*
BOTH	*Walk and talk and preach like Jesus,*
MELISSA	*And make myself rich as Croesus. They're gonna pay up, while I suffer.*
DANIEL	*I've had it tough, they'll have it tougher. I'm not proud but I'm aloof,*
MELISSA	*My reputation's bulletproof,*
BOTH	*I got those moral ascendancy blues.*
DANIEL	*(Lord have mercy!)*
BOTH	*We got those moral ascendancy, co-dependency, stick like chewing gum to your shoes, blues!*

DANIEL and MELISSA high-five, and CLEM applauds

CLEM	Shh!

Enter DAME PAMELA and EMMA

DANIEL buries himself in a music score and MELISSA hastily switches to something classical on the piano

PAMELA	If you won't get me a cab, I'll go by bus. The 268.
EMMA	Wait, you can't be tired of us already, Pam. And Charles is due back soon.
PAMELA	Two whole days! I'm not deaf to the tune you play here, a fugue in acute disdain, in smirks and sideways looks. Oh, look pained you may, you heard that jejune cabaret just now. Just the sort of trick they play. Stop it, children, be quiet if you can!
MELISSA	Ever so sorry.
DANIEL	We'll be good now, Nan.
PAMELA	'Granny', please. 'Nan' is just an affectation. They've both received a first class education and yet they try their best to emulate under-achievers from a sink estate.
MELISSA	We apologise.
DANIEL	Sincerely, *Grandmamma*.
PAMELA	If you'd struggled hard to come as far as I have come, you wouldn't think to make a joke of it. If your Dad had had to take the dole like mine, you'd *walked* to school on toast and margarine, you wouldn't laugh, or boast about a clever lyric sneering at Tartuffe.

During the next speech DANUTA enters

EMMA	Please, Pam, it's just a harmless spoof, no real malice. I really am concerned that you're offended, please don't spurn our friendship. Tartuffe's a presence here, I'll put it that way, not the easiest thing, but it's Charles's choice and we support him. We've given Tartuffe space. I've given in to his requests that *[indicating the piano]* I do no practice early in the morning, that we eat at six

	instead of eight –

Upstairs a toilet flushes

DANUTA	He go. Just like the clockwork.

PAMELA	Oh, good heavens, girl, must you always lurk? Why must this household always be so lax?

DANUTA	Beg your pardon. I order you a taxi. He text just now. He stuck in Cricklewood.

PAMELA	Oh, I see. A taxi? Well, that's good. I can wait, of course. There's a train at noon, no rush. A coffee, please. Don't forget the spoon, Danuta.

Exit DANUTA

While she's gone, I must just say
I hope you all can bring yourselves to play
a better part towards Tartuffe. You two
to treat him with the rich regard he's due
and make him truly welcome in this house.

DANIEL	That's pretty hard. He chucks his weight about like Rasputin with the Romanovs.

PAMELA	You see. Remarks like that do so make me cross! Has no-one here the grace to understand – it's vicious, envious and deeply underhand to carp, snipe and gossip about Tartuffe. He *endured* his sordid childhood. The proof is set out here so movingly in this book. Is it any wonder that the public took it to its bosom? 'Our Kid'. I grant you the title is a little mawkish, who'd deny it, but this book has taught us all how such a wretched start can be a call to arms. Did he give in, surrender hope? No, he fought his way to literacy, found scope to market mobile phones or some such thing – I'm not *au fait* with all the outs and ins – in the remotest mountains of Nepal, then gave every penny back, gave it all

away to build three schools, to make
them free from their dependency on aid.
Now here at home he's brought that clarity
of purpose to form a business charity.

CLEM A charity for business is oxymoronic.

PAMELA Ah, Clem, just like you to be ironic.
'Aspiration UK' will pass on business skills
to empower the havenots, to fulfill
their dreams. No futile handouts. It's meant
to unlock potential, harness latent talent.

CLEM Hmm. We're told about his business acumen
but doesn't it beg the question, when
this supposed financial titan stays rent free,
a guest, freeloading with impunity?
As for 'Aspiration UK', I wonder
sometimes if it's not a front for under-
world malfeasance. Guns and cocaine traded?

PAMELA Stop! This house is positively degraded
by a sort of inward-looking snobbery.
So typical you should sneer and think it robbery.

CLEM Only joking, Pam.

PAMELA In the worst of taste.
Time you grew up, Clem, if it's not too late.
Your trouble is you couldn't give a fig
about the marginalised. You're a Whig,
but deaf to anyone who doesn't share your view.
As for real experience, you haven't got a clue
about what life is like ... up north, or anywhere
that's more than the very cheapest tube fare
from Charing Cross. Parliamentary sketches?
What for? And for whom? I'm sure it fetches
you a comfortable income, but it's time
you listened to other voices, ones that chime
with this. Oh yes, you have some common sense
and you certainly keep up a good pretence
of benign humour, but at heart you're cynical.

Emotion and compassion are inimical
to you. A fact I fear your two ex-wives
discovered all too late.

CLEM   Oh, those knives
are out as well.

DANIEL   Gran, what drives me round the bend
is Tartuffe's ubiquity. Every time a friend
of ours calls round, suddenly he's there.
He's been listening from his upstairs lair.
Then when he's fixed us with his beady eye
we wilt. You hear the conversation die.

PAMELA   I expect he's being friendly, though I'm sure
he finds your friends both glib and immature.

DANIEL   More likely he's a kind of voyeur,
enjoying some secret, filthy joke.

PAMELA   That's just absurd.

DANIEL   I sometimes have to choke
back the desire to punch him in the face –

PAMELA   Daniel!

DANIEL   – just for a chance to have the place
to ourselves again. Even worse for Mel.

MELISSA   It's creepy, Gran. Soon as he hears the bell
he's down the stairs. I'm having girlfriends round,
he sits there, he doesn't make a sound,
he just leans forward. Doesn't seem to matter
however private or intimate the chatter,
he sticks it out. Sometimes, to make him go,
we pitch the chat embarrassingly low –
chlamydia, vibrators, hooky dating apps –
anything to make his will collapse,
but it's no good. And if we catch his eye
he'll turn away, as if he saw some thigh
exposed, or an inch too much of breast.

PAMELA   So, now you blame him for being modest.

He respects women. Isn't that progressive?

MELISSA   I'd call his modesty passive aggressive.

PAMELA   Listen, you two, you've had a cosy start.
             Your father has indulged you, this life apart,
             brought up here, in Hampstead Garden Suburb,
             had everything you've asked for, no need to curb
             desire – "Daddy, please I want" a refrain
             that often made your granny wince in pain –
             and now you're back again from college
             – or 'Uni', if one really must acknowledge
             that cant term – your father's paid off both your loans.
             So don't pretend you've made it on your own.
             What was it, Melissa? History of Art?
             At Exeter, of course. Is that a start
             in life? You seem to me to sit about
             and chat to friends, to preen and sigh and pout –

MELISSA   That's not fair, Gran. You know I'm going
             to start my Master's in a month.

PAMELA   Throwing
             yet more pointless debt your father's way?

MELISSA   No, not true. It's all quite clear. I'll pay
             for this. I'm not some stupid airhead, Gran,
             some dilettante. I'm sorted. When we can,
             of course, I'd like time with my fiancé, Val,
             but he's always in a whirl of work. My pals /
             make up for that –

PAMELA   A *trainee* lawyer, am I right? Your Val?

                              DANUTA brings Pamela's coffee

MELISSA   Yes, articled to a group that expedite
             the change from not-for-profits into charities.
             As moral as Tartuffe in anybody's eyes.

PAMELA   The equation's not that simple. You'll learn.
             And Dan – you're too young to marry – you'd earn
             your living as an actor, that's your aim?
             I've seen you once on stage, forget its name –

that piece of nonsense written by your friend
from Oxford, in that pub at the World's End.
The subject matter was positively obscene.
Are you too good for Ibsen, or Racine?
I suppose your ideas are too advanced
for plays that *entertain*.

CLEM   Give the boy a chance.
                At least he works and tries to pay his way.

PAMELA   I'm not against him. All I'm trying to say
                is given all the pain Tartuffe's been through
                they should acknowledge it, give the man his due.

                          Text message alert from DANUTA'S phone

                A little grace, that's all. *[To Emma]* And as for you –

EMMA   *[Aside to Clem]* For a moment I thought
                I'd got off scot-free.

CLEM   Oh no, no, you're caught.

PAMELA   Of course you have your professional life
                as a recitalist, but the best wife
                for a government minister avoids
                a big display, has the tact to deploy
                discretion, keeps in the background, out of sight.

EMMA   Pamela! You, who used to lead the fight
                for women's rights, you tell me take the veil?

PAMELA   Don't talk rot. But as a feminist curtail
                your urge to put yourself on show. To spend
                your days shopping for the bra that will lend
                you uplift, or the skirt that's far too short.
                You're not a girl, you know, you're over forty.

EMMA   Oh, thank you, Pam.

PAMELA   I'm never keen, of course,
                to make the past an issue, or to force
                comparisons that may be thought invidious,
                but their poor mama, despite her *hideous*
                taste – she was no domestic goddess –

> she did embrace the power of being modest.
> A template for the young to imitate,
> not a dish decked out to tempt inebriate
> Parliamentary colleagues at a fete.

EMMA   I beg your pardon!

CLEM   Come off it, Pam, that's just not on.

PAMELA   Oh, it's not just me that cares.
            My friend Claire Frost – *[MEL & DAN chime in with this]*
            she lives across the Square –
            said to me, in strictest confidence,
            your family seems to have lost all sense
            of decorum, that people in your position
            should be discreet.

DANUTA   Frost like the Inquisition.
            I work for her, I tell you what I know:
            face like old prune, and everything for show.
            Is nicer here, where everyone are friends.

PAMELA   She fired you. You should try to make amends.
            So wrong to attack an old employer.
            Emma, she says you soon may need a lawyer
            to deal with the tabloids. You're in their sights.
            There'll be stories – how you spend your nights.

EMMA   I'd rather you stopped, if it's all the same
            to you.

PAMELA   Of course the children are to blame.
            Dan's peculiar friends that come and go.

DANUTA   The cabbie now in Golders Green. He show
            up soon. As for Frost, she tell you lie.
            I not get fired. No, I tell you why
            I leave her house and bang my notice down:
            not bear her "put this so", her peery frown,
            "in kitchen with your coffee, girl", "don't put
            your shoes in hall", like I was dirty boy in soot
            from out your Dickens books. She is bitter,
            she is what you say a prude, and fitter

for Benedyktynki Sakramentki
House in Warsaw where old maids live and see
no young and punky people having fun.
Though not to say she living like a nun.
What she keep hidden in her knicker drawer,
if you saw you would not call her pure.

PAMELA   Ungrateful girl, that's obviously a lie,
              one which I don't propose to dignify
              with a rebuttal. Emma, I'll wait
              outside. One of you might be good and take
              my bag. A little kindness every day.

EMMA   I'll see you out.

PAMELA   That all you have to say?
              Not a word, after all the things I've said?
              Well, I suppose the family's made its bed
              and now you all must lie upon it.

              PAMELA and EMMA exit. MELISSA and DANIEL follow

CLEM   That's torn it. There's going to be a struggle.
              My brother-in-law will have to juggle
              his misplaced loyalty to that oily fraud
              upstairs and his family ties. I applaud
              the way you stood up to Dame P. just now.
              When in that mood she tends to cow
              everyone in her immediate orbit.
              We just sit back helpless and absorb it.
              Febrile English reticence. Well done you!

DANUTA   Well done Mel and Dan and Emma too.
              They not lie back flat for her attacks.
              She always like that?

CLEM   A British battle-axe?
              I suppose so, but not always in that way.
              She fought the good fight in her day.
              Workers' rights, abortion law reform,
              Tory feminist who went against the norm
              and made a difference. So depressing
              now, to see her give Tartuffe her blessing,

see her increasingly bizarre behaviour.
She really thinks the man some kind of saviour.
I need a drink. Join me in a spot of scotch,
Danuta?

DANUTA   Small one. Not drunk on job. Still got
big whole house to hoover. And then cook lunch.

CLEM pours the Glen Ord, a very large one for himself

What I think about Tartuffe – my hunch –
he hots for anything in skirt. In trousers
too, for all I know. Sight of any flesh arouse
him. He like to get your sister in the sack
maybe, for fun of paying Charlie back
for being kind and trusty. Na zdrowie!

CLEM   Na zdrowie! To Anglo-Polish amity!
I fear you could be right, you're most observant.
I wonder if, by chance, you've seen *The Servant* –
a black and white sixties classic movie?
Pretty dark, not psychedelic or groovy.
Dirk Bogarde's a manservant, name of Barrett,
corrupts his boss by means of stick and carrot –
or carrot and stick, rather. At first he seems ideal,
loyal, flattering, nothing to conceal,
but pretty soon he gets to turn the screws
in such a way that no one could accuse
him of anything in the least suspect,
but by the end the master's life is wreck'd.

DANUTA   Ah, *Sluzacy*! This I know, is film by Joseph Losey.
(*Crossing herself*) Bogarde is Satan, make himself all cosy
inside house of rich young man James Fox.
You kick out Bogarde, then you change the locks.

CLEM   Ideally, yes, that's what they ought to do.
But everything you say about Tartuffe's untrue
in Charles's mind. The wretch knows how to twist
the poor man round his finger. He won't have missed
how much he's hated by the rest of us,
but why should he give a tinker's cuss?

He can wheedle and flatter, he can charm
and play the victim, he's safe from any harm –

Enter EMMA, DAN & MELISSA. Exit DANUTA

EMMA
[to CLEM] I see you ducked her final, doorstep riff.
It's put my migraine back on track, that whiff
of cordite in the brain. Say 'Hi' for me
to Charles. He's back. I've got to see
this wretched headache off in bed before
I face the day. Sorry to be a bore.

MELISSA
Come on, Em, I'll help you get some rest.
As wicked stepmums go, you're still the best.

CLEM
I'll finish my scotch, say a brief 'hello'.
[Touching her arm] Feel better, Sis.

Exit EMMA and MELISSA

DANIEL
Clem, a private word – you know,
about this date for Mel and Val – their wedding?
Could you maybe stop Dad back-pedalling?
I'm pretty sure – of course I've got no proof –
that Dad's being leant on by the vile Tartuffe
to put the wedding off, maybe even scratch
the whole idea, persuade her Val's no match
for her. Not 'entrepreneurial' enough,
the usual creepy motivational guff
he likes to spout. I see you're not surprised?

CLEM
No, I'm afraid rather as I surmised.

DAN
Could you tackle Dad, try to put
some sense back into him? I'd put my foot
in it. Tartuffe's poisoned the well
between me and Dad. As far as I can tell
I'm rapidly becoming persona non grata.

CLEM
I'll try but I fear it's a non-starter.

DAN
Please, Clem.
It's not just for Mel, but for both of them.
Val is ace, special man. She hardly dares

to bring him home these days. A stony stare
is all he gets from you-know-who. What's happening
to us, Clem? Our life's unravelling.
We've let that insinuating shit Tartuffe
dictate to us, his word is bulletproof
where Dad's concerned. What next? Family mantras
on the need for self-reliance, or cant
debates against gay sex?

DANUTA enters with mop and bucket

CLEM   It's complex
with your Dad, you know –

DANUTA   Charles here. In hall.

DAN   I'll leave you to it. Please – he must play ball.

Exit DANIEL
Enter CHARLES

CLEM   Morning, Charles.

CHARLES   Hello, Clem. Here for lunch again?

CLEM   Yes, if that's OK? Like to check on Em,
see how she's doing, you know. Good trip?

CHARLES   Don't go, Danuta . . . *[To Clem]* With you in a tic. –
Danuta, how is everything? The family well?
– *[Back to Clem]* The conference was another empty shell,
but how things are back here is my concern.
I'm more than ever now compelled to turn
my mind to hearth and home *[back to Danuta]* –

DANUTA   Your wife, she had
headache Thursday, Friday, yes, oh so bad
and through last night. I think it still –

CHARLES   Tartuffe?

DANUTA   Tartuffe? All Thursday sunbathe on the roof,
spend hours in the shower, eat and sleep –
he's well.

CHARLES   Poor chap!

DANUTA	Friday worst. No peep from her all day. She sick and eat no food at all.
CHARLES	Tartuffe?
DANUTA	His appetite as rude as starving lion that corner antelope. He started with the paté, then he cope alone with double dover sole – his own and Mrs. Ogden's too – then he moan no enough profiterole. His hunger never stop.
CHARLES	Poor chap!
DANUTA	I give her pill but only flop on sofa, stare at ceiling in the dark.
CHARLES	And Tartuffe?
DANUTA	At ten past twelve he park his body like a shiny limousine in bed and never wake until I clean the floor real loud outside his room.
CHARLES	Poor chap.
DANUTA	At last at four or five she gets to nap – the pill it work at last – but still her head is sore, she –
CHARLES	Tartuffe, he's still in bed?
DANUTA	No. Like Phoenix he rise at bang of ten, bathe in pools of light and eat for men of army starving in the trench.
CHARLES	Poor chap!
DANUTA	So now they both are on the mend I'll tap my blind man's stick [the mop] up to her room and say you give your wife a loving kiss another day. *She exits*
CLEM	Charles, she's laughing in your face, can't you see?

And if I didn't think I'd rather weep
I'd do the same. You're like a teenage girl
trying to touch the feet of some world-
famous cokehead playing the O2.
What is it, Charles? What has got into you?
Emma's waiting for the outcome of a scan –
her constant headaches. You do understand
the seriousness – ?

CHARLES   Don't fret at that. Tartuffe
insists it'll lend his diagnosis proof:
the cause is merely psychosomatic.

CLEM   Oh yes, and when did he take the Hippocratic
Oath?

CHARLES   There's evidence these so called 'experts'
do little good, it's the bank account that hurts.
Imagine what that private doctor's fee
could have done in an underfunded charity!
Learn from him, Clem, from Tartuffe. The power
of positive thinking, not more hours
spent with quacks at some outrageous price.

CLEM   [Aside] Thank God she didn't take Tartuffe's advice. –
Though I hope I'm never quick to condemn
a man –

CHARLES   What have you got against him, Clem?

CLEM   I'll tell you what – this ghastly, *ghastly* book.
The wretched thing is everywhere you look
these days. The 'misery memoir' par
excellence. Raised in a broken-down car –

CHARLES   A caravan, a stationary caravan.

CLEM   OK. A caravan. In North Wales? Llan –
something, was it? They all begin with Llan,
don't they?

CHARLES   Prestatyn. A caravan below
the sea wall in Prestatyn. You know

the North Wales coast of course?

CLEM   OK,
point taken, I don't. But is the place
of special import? Just the clichéd slum,
rank with damp. And, of course a harlot Mum
and violent Dad. I'd give it credence,
some at least, if I'd picked up any sense
he'd ever lived a moment north or west
of Hatton Cross. You might do well to test
him on Welsh resorts, what he really knows.

CHARLES   Stop it! I will not tolerate these low
jibes about a man who's endured so much
and had the courage to reach out and touch
the world, to make them understand –

CLEM   For God's sake, Charles, misfortune is his *brand*,
his USP. His struggle out from under
his parents' grip – where are they now, I wonder?
I'd love to hear their version of the story.

CHARLES   Clem – !

CLEM   Can't you see, it's all a calculation
designed to tug the heartstrings of the nation,
perfectly calibrated on every mawkish page
to satisfy a superficial age
with titillating, hardcore misery porn,
while he sits back and lets the punters fawn.
By the way, this is a decent drop
of scotch.

CHARLES   *[Snatching the bottle]* That's Glen Ord. Ninety quid a pop.

CLEM   In that case I'll polish this last drop off.
Since when did you begin to cough
up such vast amounts of cash on booze?

CHARLES   May I not spend my money how I choose?
The fact is, Tartuffe is so ascetic
he rarely drinks, it acts as an emetic.
Yet this is one tipple he can tolerate.

CLEM	I'd no idea he was so delicate. Where is he now?
CHARLES	On Saturdays he keeps to his room sometimes, his working weeks are so demanding. And perhaps – don't smile – he finds the climate here growing hostile?
CLEM	No wonder. I gather he's not paying rent in spite of all his royalties?
CHARLES	Every cent he earns that way contributes to the cause.
CLEM	Oh, of course, the cause, how could I forget?
CHARLES	Clem, do you have to see goodness as a threat? Is there no-one you see worthy of respect, whose motives you haven't found suspect, that, living or dead, you actually admire?
CLEM	Well, if you held my feet to the fire – Attlee, Orwell, maybe Otis Redding … No, definitely Otis.
CHARLES	Don't think I don't notice how you accuse Tartuffe of feather bedding while you are happy to make free with my involuntary hospitality. If Tartuffe is culpable, so are you.
CLEM	I suppose that may be partly true. But have you checked him out, Charles? A fortune selling mobiles in the mountains of Nepal? Does that make sense? And those schools he paid for? You've phoned a Sherpa, have you, made a call or two to wish them well and ask them to corroborate that noble task?
CHARLES	That's ridiculous, and it's insulting.
CLEM	Maybe so. But this 'cause' you're funding here – 'AspirationUK.com'? An outfit he says he's converting to a charity.

<table>
<tbody>
<tr><td></td><td>You've proof of that? You've lawyers on the case?</td></tr>
<tr><td>CHARLES</td><td>Clem, these things take time! Must you debase
every honest man's attempt to change the world?
Your lip – there – so perpetually curled.
Take someone principled, idealistic,
they're 'dishonest', at best 'unrealistic'.
Your parliamentary sketches, in their way
they're witty, but you actually say
what? That peer's a crook, that MP a creep,
and the Speaker smirks like Uriah Heep?</td></tr>
<tr><td>CLEM</td><td>I'm holding them to account. It's the job
of the parliamentary sketch to dob
in any member behaving like an arse.</td></tr>
<tr><td>CHARLES</td><td>Even me, I know.</td></tr>
<tr><td>CLEM</td><td>No-one deserves a pass,
friend or foe, in power. I claim carte blanche
to excoriate you when I get the chance /
and that –</td></tr>
<tr><td>CHARLES</td><td>Not everything, everyone is rotten
to the core. And have you forgotten –
Tartuffe's outside the Westminster bubble.
He's experienced the kind of trouble
real people face. You think this book is ghastly?
Well let me tell you that you vastly
underestimate its power to motivate,
to speak to that great but voiceless estate
of folk who know they've been taken for a ride.
I was astonished, I almost cried
at what he'd written here. He'd laid bare
the manifest failure of the welfare
state. I wanted it in print, he demurred.
Eventually, he let me put a word
in in the right place. I must confess,
the fact that 'Our Kid' 's a roaring success
has given me the greatest satisfaction.
And what is more, it's stung me into action.</td></tr>
</tbody>
</table>

The new way we've designed is being assessed.
Such ambition! Even the PM's impressed.

CLEM
Why does 'new way' somehow make me shiver?

CHARLES
Perhaps because your type would never give
another voice a shout?

CLEM
Well, maybe not.
Oh, Charles, let's not both of us get hot
about all this. There's – well, Mel's engagement
to Val. What sort of arrangement
have you made?

CHARLES
Need you really interfere?

CLEM
I'm doing it for Mel, she wants you there.
There's been a strain between you two of late,
but that's no reason why she has to wait
to be happy. There's no need to frown,
it needn't turn your schedules upside down,
just name a date that suits. Mel will do the rest.
She'll be happy if you're just there to bless
her union.

CHARLES
I may have plans that I'll commune
to her in time.

CLEM
Well, they're going to do it soon,
and she'd like her family to attend.
Focus for a moment and tell them when.

CHARLES
You accept, I hope, this isn't your affair?
Comprehend, perhaps, my children's welfare
is above the pay scale of a brother-in-law?
'Wait to be happy'? What a ridiculous thought.
Mel and Dan have never had to suffer.
My wealth has always been there as a buffer.
While poor Tartuffe, despite his wretched start –

CLEM
Oh God, please, Charles!

CHARLES
– has shown he has the heart,
the character and strength to rise above

violence, cruelty and the absence of love
to seize success, become a moral force.
I know that amuses you. Of course
people like you, sophisticated, clever,
despise Tartuffe. You see his endeavour
as a trick. There's nothing more to say.
We've just come to see things in a different way.
I've admired you, no, seen you as a friend,
but this difference could truly spell the end
of our friendship, for what it's worth.

From above comes a low droning vocal sound

CLEM   This is too much! What now? What on earth – ?

CHARLES   You wouldn't understand. A spiritual exercise.
He does it for an hour to help him rise,
to focus on the task in hand, banish fears.
It's self-reliant, unlike the selfish prayers
you offer up in church. It's admirable, I think.

CHARLES exits

CLEM   This place is mad. I need another drink.

As CLEM helps himself generously from the bottle, the droning continues
Fortunately, it is soon topped by the sound of Dan & Mel singing at the
piano.

ACT TWO   11.30

Melissa is tootling at the piano. Enter Charles

CHARLES	Melissa, my dear, we … we need a chat.
MELISSA	Of course, Dad. Is something the matter?
CHARLES	I wouldn't like us to be overheard.
MELISSA	Ooh, that sounds serious. Mum's the word! It's not Emma, is it? She's not really ill?
CHARLES	Emma? No, all in the mind. Er … you will be wondering about your wedding. A date.
MELISSA	Oh, thanks, Dad! You know how much I hate to bother you, you've so much on.
CHARLES	That's not –
MELISSA	What?
CHARLES	Our family, Mel, It's always been a unit, so … so well *in tune*. Fought its battles all together. Such a strength that is, you know, to weather every storm –
MELISSA	What is it, Dad? You're nervous, that's not you. What's wrong? You always taught us to be bold.
CHARLES	Mel, there's things that I've been told … I know you think you love your Val, and he's well and good in some respects. I'm pleased to have got to know him; other cultures popping in here, keeps the tabloid vultures in their cage where race and our own record is concerned.
MELISSA	Dad?
CHARLES	Virile, too, no doubt? Affords you all a healthy, modern girl requires?

MELISSA	What? You can't say that! What on earth inspires all this? That's racist, Dad!
CHARLES	Yes, I take that back, slipped out from God knows where.
MEL	*[Aside]* I know where.
CHARLES	The truth, the fact is I want you not to marry Val.
MELISSA	What?
CHARLES	He's not for you, Mel. OK for a pal – and, as I say, he's always welcome here – but, sources tell me, since he came down last year he's 'played the field', if that's the phrase you use. While you were revising hard, eschewing all temptations, thinking of career, oh he was having fun. Oh yes, it's not gone unnoticed here. Tartuffe could fill you in.
MELISSA	I'm sure he could. No doubt list me every sin furnished by his warped imagination. How dare he interfere? Indignation's not the word, Dad –
CHARLES	Mel –
MELISSA	And who I choose to spend my life with? What's next? Refuse your blessing, like some antiquated, red-faced Presbyterian who'd rather see me dead than married to a Catholic? Isn't it for me – ?
CHARLES	Tartuffe. Tell me what you think, what you see?
MELISSA	What?
CHARLES	Tartuffe. He's been with us now all year. You've had time to size him up, get a clear impression of the man he is.
MELISSA	Well, I know how much he means to you. Honestly though –

CHARLES   He's changed my whole perspective, Mel, he's ...
          rebooted me. I sometimes can't conceive
          the man I was. Career MP, flying high
          for sure, but yet no thought of asking why,
          or what it is that we believe. Only self-
          esteem, ambition for the ermined shelf
          to snooze on when we're old. Now we've purpose
          with a heart and soul. Evangelists would call us
          'born again'. That's how I feel, though deities
          don't figure in the mix. We are the laity's
          renewal force, and we must bond as one,
          Melissa. Crusaders, if you like, bang the drum
          for a life of self-reliance, hope and moral truth.

          DANUTA enters unnoticed, again with mop and bucket

          That's why you should think about Tartuffe.

MELISSA   Think about him how?

CHARLES   Marry *him* my dear.

MELISSA   What?

CHARLES   Well?

MELISSA   I'm sorry, Dad, but did I hear ... ?

CHARLES   What?

MELISSA   Did I ... ? Who d'you think I should marry?

CHARLES   Tartuffe.

MELISSA   Tartuffe!

CHARLES   Tartuffe. Into our family.
          Just imagine it – a permanent place
          with us in this house. Together, in a space
          consecrated to our great mission. Oh
          I know he may seem far above you – no,
          no! He has noticed you, admired you, Mel,
          let me assure – What the ...? Where the hell
          did you spring from? This is a private chat.

DANUTA   I hear the strange thing in this house but – *tak!* –
              this, how you say, take the cracker.

MELISSA   Danuta –

CHARLES   It's strange, is it, to your ragbag of a mind
              that I should wish my only daughter find
              a soul-mate with whom to share her life?

DANUTA   So strange I not believe you say it. Wife
              to man who run us all around the house,
              who eat your food and drink your wine and shout
              for more till cupboard bare? It must be joke
              or you have senior minute, or you smoke
              something that make your head go –

CHARLES   Will you
              be quiet! Ignore her, Mel. I tell you who –

DANUTA   Or you be drunk. I'm not believing it.
              This is midsummer crazy. He must have fit.
              Mind gone mad like rushing train off rail
              gone bendy in bad kind of sun. I fail
              believe a word.

CHARLES   What you believe is neither
              here nor there. Please go.

DANUTA   I have to mop.

CHARLES   Either
              mop another room or take some breakfast
              to Tartuffe. You know how he is steadfast
              in his need to eat on time and well.
              We mustn't see him lose his strength or sell
              him short, the man's so precious to us all. So
              go on, jump to it, leave us. Leave us! Go!

                                        Danuta affects to exit

              Melissa, look at this with different eyes.
              Tartuffe renews our purpose, defies
              the flabby-souled passivity we've inhaled.
              From that damp and sordid caravan in Wales

	he's brought us faith, new thinking –
DANUTA	It *must be* drinking. He talk like teenage dream or senile man that walk in cloud with fairy friend and not see shit collecting on his shoe.
CHARLES	What? What is it you cannot understand? Find a tray and take some food upstairs. Break some eggs and make an omelette, brew some coffee, squeeze an orange, just leave us here to talk in peace!
DANUTA	I arrange all that two hours ago. He eat like horse, throw me back the tray (he spill the sauce), then tell me come downstairs and mop the floor like he was boss man here.
CHARLES	Well, you can be sure he only wanted to be certain you were using time I pay for – generously – to the best advantage. Now please mop or sweep another room.
DANUTA	I done them all. I keep my earphones in, not hear your funny chat. Ignore Danuta. Pretend I only cat asleep on sofa while you persuade your Mel to marry with the creepy guest from hell.

She plugs her earphones in

CHARLES	How dare you – ! Mel, it's very hard to … She really gets my goat, that girl, she's like a limpet, no a *limpet mine*, clinging to this fantastic ship we're sailing into new and undiscovered waters.
MELISSA	Dad –
CHARLES	Ignore her, Mel, let's both ignore her.

Danuta sings

	Oh, for God's sake!

DANUTA   *[Loud over song in her ears]* A lovely, soppy song!
            Young pair make love and run away, along
            from home a hundred mile. I shut up now.

CHARLES   I – ! Can she hear us, Mel? It's this, it's how
            we live, we reconceive and reconstruct
            our mode of life. Tartuffe, you know, has plucked
            us out of nowhere. Yes, I know I'm *known* –
            perhaps a rising star, waiting for a phone-
            call from the PM – don't put that about,
            may come to nothing – but there's no doubt,
            I've been chosen!

MELISSA   By the PM?

CHARLES   By Tartuffe!
            His commitment here, his love. The proof
            is in the sacrifice he's made to live
            with us and share what he can give
            the nation, Mel. Tartuffe will be the lead, tease
            us from our slack dependencies, release
            our full potential, make us citizens
            of a world in which –

DANUTA   You live in caravan
            or in cardboard box below the bridge
            while man on second floor he raid your fridge
            and laugh all way to bank. He fraud that man!

CHARLES   I am exercising patience here, Danuta,
            but I will not very long. Tartuffe is
            humble and sincere, a victim of misfortune
            that *might* have made him what you say / but –

DANUTA   You blind? You mad? I take him food, I lay
            his clothes out nice on bed, I pick his rubbish
            off the floor (he pinch my bum like I his dish,
            you say, or whore?). Never he say thanks for it
            or make –

CHARLES   I warn you, I will not permit –

DANUTA

No, you listen me. You think Tarfuffe
is what you call 'a gentleman'? Is proof
he always take his shower when I clean
and let his towel slip, make sure I seen
his private part he wave about I think
for me to blush while he make smile and wink
me like he have the biggest prick in town?
You good man, Charles, Tartuffe he bring you down,
he, how you say, take you for a riding,
live here, spend your money, you providing
everything he need like he a starving
beggar from Mumbai! He make my blood boil
and you want your daughter Mel to spoil
her life –

CHARLES

Oh, can't you rant! A Polish peasant
with a Mickey Mouse degree in patent
ways to read the stars!

DANUTA

In *astrophysic*
my degree, from Cracow / University.

CHARLES

How dare you stick
your oar in all the time! You're paid to cook and clean,
not grace us with your thoughts or vent your spleen.
And for your *work* – I'll tell you now – we hate
the stink of bleach that greets us at the gate
and tracks us round the house like broken wind.
And for your cooking, an undisciplined
infant could construct a better menu
to sustain hard-working people through
a busy week. Fish on *every* Friday – God,
the Pope himself, I'm sure, has missed the odd
one in his life! And if I hear you mangle
English grammar one more time I might just strangle
you at dawn! Get out, get out, get out!

MELISSA

Dad – !

CHARLES

You be quiet, too! This woman makes me mad!
If it wouldn't be tabloid food and drink I'd sack

	her on the spot and see her hurried back to Poland!

MELISSA   I can't believe I'm hearing this!

CHARLES   Then listen harder. Perhaps you'll get the gist.
           Wed your Val, if you must. On any date you choose.
           I won't be there, nor Emma, nor anyone who's
           respect for me or for this house. Think on
           Tartuffe, Melissa, or pack your bags, begone.

                                                      He exits

DANUTA   I think I time my entrance very bad.

MELISSA   Danuta, did my Dad
           say all that? Am I awake? Bad enough
           to chuck me out, but all that crazy stuff
           he said to you. I'm sorry, I'm ashamed.

DANUTA   He not himself. Sick virus in the brain.
           Blame Emperor live on second floor.

MELISSA   Shit, can't you ever get it right – the floor?

DANUTA   Sorry, what?

MELISSA   Ground floor, first floor! Tartuffe's
           apartment's on the first. The bloody roof's
           where he belongs. No, tethered in the cellar,
           the troglodyte from hell who's never
           ever going to leave us. Oh God, I'm
           sorry, sorry …

DANUTA   Sokay, Mel. This bad time
           for all you people in this house, like it been –
           [offering cloth] here, only dust a bit with it, it clean –
           like it not your own, like foreign army try
           to turn it into barracks. But no need you cry.

MELISSA   Easy to say that. But what am I to do?

DANUTA   Your life your own. Not marry to please fool
           you call your Dad. Tell him he should marry
           with Tartuffe, pick him up and carry
           him through door like love's young dream. You marry Val.

A pause

My parents poor. They want me marry well,
not go to university, not think 'career'.
And maybe they were right. I end up here
and with degree – *my PhD!* – in astrophysic
cook and clean and sometime make you sick
with stink of bleach. You love him well, I guess.

MELISSA   My Dad? Of course.

DANUTA   I mean your Val.

MELISSA   Oh. Oh yes,
I love him very much.

DANUTA   And he loves you?

MELISSA   He does. No doubt at all for nearly two
years on either side. Not fashionable
I know to be quite so keen on stable
twosome at young age. God, I start talk like
Polish girl who get by well in English, 'spite
she never learn her past from present tense.

DANUTA   My tenses never stop me seeing sense.
So you in love with Val. What problem is there?

MELISSA   I think I'm in a state of shock. I never
thought I'd hear my father talk like that,
or think like that, or be like that.
I rather think I'd like to kill myself.

DANUTA   Oh, good! You solve it well. This little elf,
this tiny, peasant brain not think of that.
Just die, and Val and Tartuffe fight like cat
together on your grave. Like Hamlet and
the other one – forget his name – the man
who poison sword at end of play. Good Polish
film in that, big hole in ground, soulish wind –

MELISSA   Oh, do shut up! Or tell me what to do!

DANUTA   *[Shrugging]* You marry Val.

MELISSA   About my Dad! Don't tell me you
               can't see I have a problem here? My Dad's
               besotted with these daft ideas, these mad,
               completely insubstantial dreams that fraud
               Tartuffe has – God, I'd like a poisoned sword
               to stick up his fat arse! My Dad's a minister
               of state! It's weird, Danuta, it's sinister
               the way Tartuffe is making him a fool.

DANUTA   Your Dad is good man, Mel, I know you'll
               see him, how you say, himself again in week
               or two. Don't fret the things he say to me.
               He kind to me when I arrive from frosty
               woman cross the square, he pleased with
               how I speak and cook. I like him, only he
               not laugh at life no more, and only see
               Tartuffe. Soon he shut the door on him
               and like your Val again.

MELISSA   You're sure of that?

DANUTA   I stake my PhD. Eat up my hat.
               Go, make yourself look nice, call up Val,
               have lunch somewhere, tell him he have rival
               in Tartuffe.

VAL   [Off] Melissa!

DANUTA   He here. Go give him kiss.
               He clever boy, he laugh like sink at this.

                                        Exit DANUTA. Enter VAL

MELISSA   Val, thank God, thank God you're here!

VAL   Really? That's strange. I'm surplus, so I hear,
               to your requirements. Learnt it from the cat,
               I think, or was it a post-it note on that fat
               Buddha in the hall? The means is immaterial –

MELISSA   Val, what's this?

VAL   – It's like some trashy serial,
               the cheapest kind of soap, credits rolling

	even now, but there's no breathless waiting for the sequel if you're me. Bloody hell, how could you be so devious, Mel?
MELISSA	Val?
VAL	I thought you were the real McCoy, heart, integrity, on top of looks. A joy-filled inventory of all that's good. It's certain is it, this?
MELISSA	Val, I – I can see you're hurt but tell me, what – ?
VAL	Oh, don't go all artless now. Your marriage to Tartuffe, you cow!
MELISSA	Marriage – ! Well, since you mention it, though I won't pretend I like your tone –
VAL	My tone? You don't –
MELISSA	My father has conveyed the feelings of his friend that he, Tartuffe, was reticent to send to me himself –
VAL	Reticent – Tartuffe? He wouldn't shrink from telling Jesus when to pee! More front than José Mourinho. But fine, go on, count up his value against mine. His book, that's making millions, his fame, his entrée to the smartest set, his game of *spot the sitting duck*. I'm a swimmer, not a bad one, but so what? I've a glimmer that my rented, one bed flat in Kilburn Park's not good enough for the daughter of the patriarch of new-world shit. You're set on this?
MELISSA	Not quite. What would you advise?
VAL	What, me?
MELISSA	Yes. What would you suggest?
VAL	Why ask me?

MELISSA   Because you're here, I guess.
               And seem to have a lot to say. So on,
               help me to decide, there's no forgone
               conclusion here. Give me the best of your
               brilliant legal mind. Should I tie the knot?

VAL   Then yes, indeed. Go marry him, why not?

MELISSA   You mean that?

VAL   I do! *Tartuffe*? Phew, a catch!
               Grab him before some better options hatch
               in his sordid, grasping mind, he thinks again.

MELISSA   OK, I will.

VAL   Good!

MELISSA   Good!

VAL   That's sorted then.
               I'll have that ring if that's OK. Worth
               a few more games from ebay. The dearth
               of other things to do, you know, to while
               away the evenings on your own. Don't smile,
               you snake! You underhand, you sly and grasping shit,
               you never loved me, I should have known it
               couldn't be for real. How could it be?

MELISSA   Well, think that if you like! Go on, feel free
               to say some more. This bile's been boiling,
               I'm in awe! I don't remember 'snake' taking
               part in foreplay – not that you'd much time for that,
               too keen to make me squeak 'Ooh Val!' –
               or 'sly', or 'shit', or 'underhand'. Are there
               any other insults you would like to air
               to show how much you really hated me,
               held me in contempt while you parked your perky
               little vehicle up my street?

VAL   Don't turn
               this all on me! You're the one who's worming
               out of this, who's showing me the door.

MELISSA	I'm not! I'm …Oh, this is stupid, Val. I'm sure I've no idea how … Please, Val, please we can't …
VAL	Go on like this? No, *Mel*, we bloody can't. I've never been so humiliated. Are you so thick-skinned you fail to – no, you'll never know it, will you, the Ogden silver spoon! – to see what this is like, what it *feels like* for me?
MELISSA	I was trying to say, Val, trying to say …
VAL	Not trying hard enough. Trust a blasé child of Ogden, fat cat, snob and just-born again disciple of Tartuffe's tawdry sideshow –
MELISSA	Right, that's it. Get out! I never want to see you here again! Not ever, Val!
VAL	You mean that?
MELISSA	Yes!
VAL	Really?
MELISSA	Yes. Yes. I – Oh, go, go, please go, now Val, please, goodbye!

MEL collapses on the sofa, head in hands
VAL stares at her for a second and then leaves
The sound of Dan & Mel singing again as the lights go
down.

ACT THREE   12.30

Charles' annotated copy of 'Our Kid' sits on the piano or a table
Sound of hoovering off. Enter TARTUFFE from the garden, carrying
two bottles of water. After a few moments, a puffing CHARLES
enters in lycra jogging kit. TARTUFFE gives him a water bottle, but
before he can enjoy it ...

TARTUFFE   Wait Charles, complete the celebration
                of our purpose. Let's make the salutation
                in saying our mantra. Inner strength and calm.

TARTUFFE stands straight, raises his hands in prayer. CHARLES follows
his example

                (*Chanting*) Vahaan ek har minat ka janm.

CHARLES   (*Chanting*) Vahaan ek har minat ka janm.

                TARTUFFE stretches out his arms and waggles his fingers

TARTUFFE   Now let your energy forth into the strata
                (*Chanting*) Chutiya, chutiya.

CHARLES   (*Chanting*) Chutiya, chutiya.

                They bow to each other. CHARLES at last gets a drink

                Thank you, my friend. I feel so full of vigour.

TARTUFFE   Of course. You're match fit for the bigger
                challenge now. I see a natural leader,
                swimming above the average bottom feeder
                or political plankton. You're the pilot whale,
                the master of the ocean, showing us the way.

CHARLES   Well, yes, I feel ... it could be as you say.
                That martial art you were teaching me,
                I wonder –

TARTUFFE   I'm glad you asked. 'Hap Chi'.
                I learnt it in those mountains in Nepal,
                from a Hap Chi master. Some precious crumbs
                of wisdom from his table.

CHARLES   I'm all-thumbs.

TARTUFFE   Forget your hands and learn to use your feet.

The well-judged kick that aims to meet
your foe's *upastha*, seat of reproduction,
will achieve the complete destruction
of the essence of the wiliest opponent.

CHARLES   That seems, you know, somehow rather violent.

TARTUFFE   What? Oh no. It's a form of respect.
You understand, and thereby deflect
the negative impulse of your foe.
To make him helpless is to truly know
him. In business, more than self-defence,
it's communication, focused, pure, intense.
But the main thing, Charles, you must remember,
whales and bottom-feeders, we two number
among the whales. That's the *aspirational*
way, that's the selfish *and* the selfless, *moral*
way to go. Whales –

CHARLES   – and bottom-feeders.
Yes, that's so profound. Though I may just need
a clearer steer on it, a preciser line
perhaps … ?

TARTUFFE   No, no, you're there. I know you're fine.
Charles, don't let the plankton undermine
your inner strength. Alone on a mountain in Nepal –
I'd made a fortune, and given it all
away, I had nothing – but in that golden hour
I knew for certain: we are our own higher power.

CHARLES   Gosh, I remember *[picking up 'Our Kid']* – page 94 was it?
Maybe 93. Your epiphany …

TARTUFFE   Giving everything away sets us free.

CHARLES   I understand – I think. So much I have to learn.

TARTUFFE   Charles, it's me that learns from you. I discern
an inner drive in you, a will of ice.

CHARLES   Oh, well …

TARTUFFE   But did you follow my advice
                in abstaining from all intimacy –
                the indulgence of *sambhoga* with your wife?

CHARLES   As a matter of fact these days my life
                is so hectic, there's little opportunity,
                but it's hard –

TARTUFFE   You haven't learned immunity
                from the pull of sex? The castrati
                in their condition produced the purest art.

CHARLES   Good God, Tartuffe, you're not suggesting –

TARTUFFE   No, no, I just don't want you investing
                vital energy in physical desire.

CHARLES   I love her, you see. I can't put out the fire
                just like that.

TARTUFFE   I'm not an autocrat
                and not a saint, yet I've been celibate
                for five long years. But I won't dictate
                what you should or shouldn't do.
                You must only do what seems right to you.

CHARLES   Yes, that's right, yes, I do understand.
                I'll make more effort, use more self-command.
                God, that conference in Scotland was maddening,
                I see things so clearly now, so saddening
                to hear the same, unexamined shibboleths
                bandied back and forth, no will to test
                assumptions or to think anew. Thank God
                for 'Our Kid'. I read it in every odd
                moment I could find – the fourth time now –
                in breaks, then on the sleeper coming down
                from Perth. In every read it shows me more,
                so rich, so subtle, and at the same time *raw*.
                This time, just coming through Carlisle,
                I turned again to that bruising though beguiling
                afternoon in Widnes, that Damascene
                moment when you saw that hapless teen-

age child so savagely assaulted
by its Mum. Distressed but then exalted
– it's here – page sixty-one, I made
a note …

TARTUFFE   That's kind.

CHARLES   Yes, you were quite remade
by that event. At only fifteen years of age
you saw your way! I admit I shed a tear.
It affected me so much I almost couldn't bear
to carry on. I nearly shut the book,
sat there, an idiot, while my shoulders shook.

TARTUFFE   Charles, listen, you must never be afraid
to cry in public. If your grief's displayed
it's just more honest. Everyone can see
and share the moment. That's what set me free.

CHARLES   That's very wise.

TARTUFFE   My journey's been incredible, it's true,
though there were things that I was made to do
I don't think I could even now make known.
A part of me forever just my own,
a private well filled up with guilt and fear.

CHARLES   Not help to share the burden – let me hear … ?

TARTUFFE   You may be right. [Pause] So many painful times,
humiliations, and petty crimes.
I wonder if you could understand the shame.
Once when my mam was out there on the game
I caught my Dad dolled up in one of her frocks.

CHARLES   My God!

TARTUFFE   He knocked me down and dragged me to the docks.

CHARLES   You walked like that, him en déshabillé?

TARTUFFE   You what?

CHARLES   I mean with him got up that way.

TARTUFFE	Oh no. He stole a car. He made *me* steal it. The shame of that. Even now I feel it.
CHARLES	Dreadful. How on earth did you survive?
TARTUFFE	At last we found some filthy back street dive. I had to watch him lisp and mince and croon – drunk, maudlin, madly out of tune – yelled " 'Ere, our kid, pass around the hat for contributions!" It never came to that. I remember the song – *(Crooning)* "How are things in Glocca Morra".
CHARLES	From Brigadoon?
TARTUFFE	Mmm. The men were brutes but felt some moral horror. They beat him up and threw him on the street.
CHARLES	My poor friend, how could they cheat you of your childhood so?
TARTUFFE	I don't know. *[Choking]* Imagine, my sole role model lying in a stupor in a puddle. Charles, you're like the father I never had.
CHARLES	Oh, dear boy.
TARTUFFE	*[Crying out]* Dad! <div align="right">*He embraces CHARLES*</div>
CHARLES	Whatever life threw at you, you were equal to it.
TARTUFFE	I suppose it could go in a sequel, that story. Alone it's worth a chapter.
CHARLES	I've had a thought, with the right adapter 'Our Kid' would translate brilliantly to the screen. Remember that remarkably haunting scene – your mam in bed with her latest so called beau? You describe – quite beautifully – how a glow suffused the caravan, caused by the static

from the nylon sheets. It's really cinematic.

TARTUFFE   Only if the director really understood
            my journey. Perhaps Jude Law could
            play me as an adult – if the rights were sold?

CHARLES   Brilliant casting!

TARTUFFE   Maybe. Not too old?

CHARLES   Oh for heaven's sake – Danuta!

DANUTA   *[Off]* I come!

CHARLES   That noise! Surely it should be done
            by now!

> The hoovering stops. Enter DANUTA. Open
> shirt, knotted below her bra, low-cut jeans

            Tartuffe and I are trying
            to talk. Could you kindly move your hoovering
            elsewhere?

DANUTA   OK. I empty bins instead.

> She bends down to reach one

CHARLES   And – oh I say – this really must be said –
            I'm sure, Tartuffe here would agree – your dress?

TARTUFFE   Oh, yes.

CHARLES   A little more discretion, just a little less
            on show? The dignity of womanhood
            is a thing we must restore, we should
            perhaps rewind the spool to a more austere
            age, agree?

DANUTA   Perhaps you like me here
            to cover badly with a towel instead?

CHARLES   I'm at a loss to grasp your point. Not *shed*
            your clothes, but cover up, be more discreet.

TARTUFFE   In language too, Danuta. Don't compete
            for a distinguished man's attention by
            simply showing off.

CHARLES   Perhaps you could apply
                 yourself to lunch? I think I heard Val leave
                 which makes the party – um – six, I believe.
                 Just a salad and some cold meats, no wine.
                 My children drink far too much, combine
                 beer and wine with God knows what. Danuta, please?

DANUTA   OK, I go. Your distinguished guest, he's
                 happy with salad lunch, no booze? I see
                 no lick his lips.

CHARLES   That's quite enough, Danuta. Go.

                                                    Danuta exits

                 That girl's a trial to us all. Got no
                 shred of sense of when to speak, when to hold
                 her tongue.

                           The hoover starts up again – a quick blast

                 Danut – ! Why, only an hour ago
                 she butted in when I was – actually, that's
                 a thing we must discuss, because the fat's
                 in the fire where Melissa is concerned.
                 My approach on your behalf was spurned
                 with some – well, vigour, you might say – and there's
                 no doubt your work's cut out if you're to fare
                 much better on your own behalf.

TARTUFFE   My feelings
                 for Melissa, though they're deepening
                 every hour – her suppleness of mind,
                 her music, that *modesty* we so rarely find,
                 affect me so that I could almost lose
                 my sense of purpose – Charles, do not abuse
                 the delicacy of her feelings, that
                 uniquely calibrated fabric
                 of desire we call the heart to foist an
                 unwelcome, unattractive, harsh-voiced man
                 like me upon her.

CHARLES   Dear chap, you cannot –

TARTUFFE   No, Charles, no. I will extinguish, quite blot

out unreciprocated love. My over-
whelming wish is that 'Casanova
Val' she sees for what he is. I recoil
from criticising character, or spoiling
any woman's thoughts of any man, but *Val* –
the stories I have heard I doubt if I shall
ever fail to shudder when I think of Mel,
our dear, dear Mel, succumbing to the spell
of such a dissolute, dissimulating
rogue.

CHARLES   Dear boy, of course I know your thinking
is typically unselfish and apposite.
I know no jealousies or shrill, dishonest
motive ever moves you. I will use what
influence I have. My debt to you I'll not
attempt to weigh. Every day it grows
more great. Lunch is soon, but first I'll go
upstairs with this, start again at chapter
one, 'Beginnings'. Could any title now be apter?

Exit CHARLES. TARTUFFE reflects a
moment and then exits by another door

DANUTA   *[Off]* Keep hands yourself, dirty man! Odpieprz się!

A note or two from the piano for a brief time-lapse

Enter DANIEL and CLEM

DANIEL   This is the bloody limit, Clem. I swear
I'll cut his bollocks off, fry them, ram the pair
of them down his throat until he chokes.
Marry Mel? She'd rather sell herself to blokes
at twenty quid a time than hit the sack
with that disgusting heap of monomatic,
self-advertising / oily –

CLEM   Dan, take a breath. You know damn
well that Mel would never dream of such a thing.
This is just another madness promising
to derail your Dad's career. You won't help him
by getting all steamed up and threatening

medieval quarterings.

DANIEL
Well, maybe not,
but a punch in the nose or a mighty swat
across his arse might do the trick and make
him sling his hook.

CLEM
Oh Dan, please, for God's sake
talk like a grown-up. Great story for the hacks –
"son of junior Minister attacks
celebrated business guru". Anyway,
fisticuffs, believe me, isn't you. Stay
out of this, my sister can allay
all fears, I know, and knock this nonsense
on the head, this ridiculous pretence
that Mel will fall into Tartuffe's arms after
fatherly advice. You'd hear the laughter
from here to Notting Hill. Em is coming down,
she's going to tackle Tartuffe now,
so let's both hop it and allow her space
to operate.

DANIEL
Not me, I'm staying to face
the viper down, lend Em some steel and grit.
A silent backup if you like, poised to land a hit –

CLEM
Dan, no! Trust Em to use her charms. I hear
them on the stairs. Try not to appear
an avenging angel. Go and get some air!

*CLEM watches as DANIEL
heads for the French windows, then exits. DANIEL turns back and
hides behind the Chesterfield*

EMMA
[Off] This room will be quiet. I'd like to have a

Enter EMMA and TARTUFFE

private word with you, Tartuffe, about a
rather delicate matter …

TARTUFFE
I obey
your every wish. You know in what regard
I hold you, Emma.

EMMA   Thanks. I have been hard
                on you on one or two occasions. Peace
                is difficult to maintain, I find, at least
                in a busy household, young things returning
                to the nest from Uni, both scattering
                chaos around the house, the strain is prone
                to show. I'm sorry if I've seemed a stony-
                faced hostess to you, perhaps, at times.

TARTUFFE   Not a shadow of that thought has crossed my mind.
                I see an ironic smile when over dinner
                I insist we must reveal our inner-
                most ambitions for the cause, break free
                from inhibition. You smile now, you see!
                I amuse you. For you it's just a game.

EMMA   It's just – I can't take seriously your name.
                Why on earth 'Tartuffe'? Where's that come from?
                What's wrong with Reg or Kevin, Mike or Tom?

TARTUFFE   You don't know that, you haven't read 'Our Kid'.

EMMA   That's not fair, I meant to, well I did,
                or rather if I'm truthful, dipped in and out.
                I do know that your father was a lout
                but, to be honest, the rest was heavy going.

TARTUFFE   I respect you, Emma, for showing
                such honesty. I'll tell you why I call myself
                'Tartuffe'. I saw one, standing on a shelf
                in a cake shop.

EMMA   Really?

TARTUFFE   Yes. Mam and I
                had gone to Bangor, a place she often plied
                her trade, dolled up in PVC and lycra.
                She went off with a rep in his Nissan Micra,
                dumped me by this shop to keep me occupied.
                You can't know how hunger gnaws at your inside
                when you see food that's just out of reach.
                And there was that tartuffe, chocolate and peach

and topped with cream. Asked if I could have it.
"Two quid" she said. "Oh, I hoped you'd give it",
I said as sweetly as I could, "I've no money."
"Clear off before I belt you! Think you're funny, sonny?"
I vowed one day I'd go back to Bangor,
claim that cake to make up for my anger
about everything in my childhood.

EMMA Under the circumstances I suppose you would.

TARTUFFE From that day on I'd only answer to
'Tartuffe'. Of course nobody but me knew
why I chose that name and what it meant.
For me it was a symbol of attainment.
It set me free.

EMMA Isn't a 'tartuffe' a fungus?

TARTUFFE *[Distracted]* Sorry?

EMMA Anyway, here you are – among us –
and while you're here, I need your advice.
It seems Melissa may have to pay the price
for her doting father's new-found zeal.

TARTUFFE First, Emma, let me tell you that I feel
your sickness – your migraines – as my own.
And while I'm here, know – you're not alone.

EMMA Well, I've seen a specialist, as you know.
I've had the scans. We'll see what they show.

TARTUFFE If you'll forgive me, I think that your mistake
is to put your faith in experts. The ache
you feel is more of the spirit than the head.

EMMA I don't want to talk about this. As I said
my concern at this moment is with Mel.

TARTUFFE Emma, Emma, let a dear friend tell
you, western medicine has failed to comprehend
the many different routes that healing lends.
There's something so much finer I would love
to try if you'll permit my practised touch?

EMMA	Not my scene, no thanks.
TARTUFFE	Dear Emma, seemingly serene yet so up-tight. Let me enlighten you. Close your eyes, imagine you're a speck, drifting –
EMMA	*[Breaking away]* I have migraines, not a stiff neck. About Mel, this absurd idea you marry her.
TARTUFFE	Don't you feel marriage is, deep down, a barrier to true communication? On some deeper plane we are all married to each other. Let me explain about inhibition: your migraines may be caused by frustration, now that Charles has paused performance of conjugal duties.
EMMA	What?
TARTUFFE	It's my understanding that you're not getting any physical satisfaction from poor Charles. A distinct lack of action, in bed, no Ogden-style seduction.
EMMA	Exactly how did you make that deduction?
TARTUFFE	I sense it. The vibrations that emanate from you –
EMMA	For fuck's sake, what?
TARTUFFE	They're palpable. Don't deny them, Em, don't wait. I could cure your illness more effectively in bed, ditch your inhibitions, tear out every shred of guilt, repression. The sex you've missed should be right at the top of your bucket list.
EMMA	Good God! Is this the sordid sequel to your book? Another new departure, equal in depravity to the sheerest saintliness your teenage mind professed to find on – when was it now – a wet and windy day in Widnes? I read that bit. What happened to Mr. Compassion?

TARTUFFE	Out of fashion, replaced by a Tantric master of the carnal arts. The fact is I see the way you clock Mel's virile friends when Charles is not around, the looks you lend across the room. You're gagging for it, Emma. Charles hasn't got the will, or the stamina, so let me show you true erotic power, show you I can keep it up for hours. *A brief pause*
EMMA	May I correct one detail in this scenario, interject one tiny cavil? Charles propped up in bed, reading Wisden in his flannel pyjamas is more erotic than this trashy drama you've got up, this tacky Soho farce.
TARTUFFE	You bitch! Think you can sneer because you're rich? You're just a frigid snob.
EMMA	And you're a knob. Now, 'Tartuffe', I could I suppose speak of this to Charles direct, or let it leak out slowly somehow, how you've behaved, but I think the news you're *so* depraved he might find humiliating, given the passion with which he's fallen for your fashion- able, mystic-motivational crap. So here's a deal. Say some 'family mishap' requires you back in Wales, leave no address, and I swear I'll never / breathe a word –
DANIEL	*[Emerging]* Em, don't mess with any thought but this – expose him now. We've got him!
EMMA	Daniel?
DANIEL	Can you believe all that? Every word I heard. Seduce my Dad's beloved wife, would you, you slimy groper, you misogynistic creep?

EMMA	Daniel –
DANIEL	Don't let him off the hook. Don't sweep this under the carpet. Every syllable I've committed to my memory. I'm able, being an actor, to deploy mnemonic skill. *[Aside]* The fact the bastard spoke in rhyme will help.
EMMA	Daniel, no! Don't put your father through this. And shame on you for spying like that on us. If the puffball here agrees my terms, we draw a line, put him, 'Our Kid', and any nonsense more out of sight and out of mind.
DANIEL	What? He's tried to ruin my sister's life – and yours. He's lied to Dad –
EMMA	You'll make us all a laughing-stock unless you get a grip, see sense and knock your indignation on the head.
DANIEL	I see the situation clearly, Em, that he – this hypocrite who's hoodwinked not just us but half the British public – that he must be exposed. Our solemn duty, no debate. Here comes Dad.
	Enter CHARLES
EMMA	Oh, God!
CHARLES	Hullo. I almost ate alone. What's going on?
EMMA	Sorry, dear, I can't –
	EMMA exits
CHARLES	Emma, what's up, my dear? It's clear that something is. Tartuffe, please fill me in.
DANIEL	I think it might be best if I begin? Dad, your guest, this creature here you style

a secular saint I've witnessed try
to get your wife, dear Emma, into bed!
No blush, no trace of shame, some threadbare
bullshit to begin, then this quite obscene,
creepy claim that he's a sex machine, as if
this were some cruddy singles venue, stiff
with lonely housewives craving any man
who'd give them time of day. She put him bang
to rights, I'll give her that – I never dreamt
she could be so frank! I managed to pre-empt
her offer to the snake to hush the whole
thing up. Dad, we've – now his cover's blown –
we've got to publish his hypocrisy, dish him
in the tabloids, and the Telegraph, get Clem –

CHARLES
Stop! Now! Be quiet! Tartuffe, can there
be any truth in this, contemplate an affair … ?

TARTUFFE
Charles, unhappily every word that Daniel's said
is true. I might protest that 'getting into bed'
does misrepresent the completeness
of my passion for your wife, but confess
to it, I must. I have been helpless, Charles.
Her purity, so foreign to my heart –
you know my experience of womanhood's
so damaged, so debased it's never stood
me well – she's, completely uninvited,
and innocently too, of course, lighted
up my soul. What can I say? I must go,
of course, and I deserve every show
of shame, every front page exposé
that Dan desires. My dream – Aspiration UK –
well, it's bust, and I must reconcile
myself to humbler work. High profile
stuff, I guess it's not for me –

CHARLES
Wait, Tartuffe.
Are you completely blind? Daniel, is the truth
of this so obscure to you?

DANIEL
What on earth – ?

CHARLES   Don't interrupt. How dare you vilify
             this good-hearted man?

DANIEL   Good-hearted? I – I
             can't believe you're saying that. He's taken
             you for a fool, Dad. Will you never waken
             up and see –

CHARLES   Dan, be careful what you say.
             I won't be called a fool or disobeyed
             by an immature young boy who thinks he's
             morally superior –

TARTUFFE   Charles, listen, please!
             Let Daniel speak. He's right. Call Clem,
             tell him every sordid detail, he'll pen
             it well and yet see that you and Em
             come through with dignity intact. He'll stem
             all whiff of foolishness, naiveté.
             Only I should pay the price.

CHARLES   [To Daniel] Now, you say … ?

DANIEL   Dad, he's bluffing, you can't believe this stuff!

CHARLES   Oh for God's sake Daniel, that's enough!
             Yes, Tartuffe's addresses to your mother are –
             well, inappropriate, of course, and hardly
             what one expects of an honoured guest,
             but a momentary lapse, prompted by a quest
             for love, the kind of which you know so well
             he's missed throughout his life, doesn't spell
             betrayal –

TARTUFFE   Charles –

CHARLES   No, let me speak my mind.
             See it as a *compliment* to Emma, a
             recognition of her warmth, her array
             of talents, her integrity, her *beauty*, Dan.
             Dear boy, we must see clearly, understand
             just how important it is now to cut
             our friend a little slack, not try to gut him

	like a fish you've landed in your net.
DANIEL	I'm speechless. Was I on another planet? I didn't hear 'our friend' declare your Emma 'gagging for it' or that you, Dad, you lacked the 'stamina' to – well, so caught in your career you couldn't –
CHARLES	That's enough! I will not hear another word. You want him out, you're jealous, want to alienate, drive a wedge between us. Well, you won't. Tartuffe and I, we have plans against which all this petty sniping ranks as odious as any parliamentary back-stabbing I recall. You haven't any more to say, I trust. You've friends whose floors will welcome you, no doubt, because these doors are shut on you, Daniel, pack your things –
TARTUFFE	Charles, this is harsh –
CHARLES	Don't interfere. Managing my family is my prerogative. Apologise without condition or live elsewhere until you've seen the shaming error –
DANIEL	Apologise, can you be kidding? To this manipulative creep? I'd rather stick my hand in puss, spit blood, or smother my head in diesel oil.
CHARLES	For God's sake, out! Not another idiotic word, I'll clout you, I swear I will, if you speak again.

A momentary pause

| DANIEL | Jesus Christ! |

DAN exits

| TARTUFFE | Charles, I am completely mortified by this. This rupture in your family, this pain is down to me, my presence here at least. |

I must leave. If I can duck Dan's tabloid feast
of righteous indignation I'll pursue
our plans alone, if not I'll find some new
way to survive.

CHARLES   My dearest friend, don't dream
of giving up the cause. It's the theme
I've looked for all my political life.
And your place is here.

TARTUFFE   But they hate me. Wife
son, daughter, all despise me and look to
rubbish all my work, 'Our Kid' – the book you
so generously encouraged me to write.
And can I really stay here out of sight
of Emma? You could hardly wish that I
had contact with her now, the writing's
surely on the wall in that respect.

CHARLES   No, no,
that's not my way at all. We strike a blow
for truth and openness, defy all scandal,
live on as we do, that's the way to handle
the sullen look, the meretricious slur.
Don't avoid my wife. Spend time with her,
dine with her, be seen with her around,
that's the proper – and the clever – way to drown
suspicion.

TARTUFFE   Charles, your wisdom, and compassion,
they're beyond praise. In a spirit of contrition
I'll do exactly as you wish. I – I –
I can't, I don't know how …

CHARLES   Don't be afraid to cry,
you told me that yourself. Here's a napkin,
filched, I'm afraid, from the buffet chap in
first class on the train from Perth. Not quite
a duck house, is it, but I daresay not right
in the eyes of Branson. Should I bribe him
with a Commons teaspoon, or cup, d'you think?

TARTUFFE   That's very funny, Charles, good chap you are.

CHARLES   Well, maybe. But through this silly – hoohah
                I've begun to see my way. While Daniel
                made me wild I'm so much cooler now. You'll
                find that my commitment to our cause
                will be redoubled, there'll be no further pause
                in forward planning. I'm going to give –
                give Aspiration UK – this house. We can live,
                have all we need, Em and I, in the flat
                that comes with my constituency. That's
                the way to go, downsize, let the cause enjoy
                a house here in the Suburb. Annoy
                the Residents Association I've no doubt
                but we lay down a signal marker, set out
                our stall by this – this petty sacrifice.
                It would have gone to Dan and Mel, suffice
                to set them up for life, but they've no need
                of feather-bedding, they've the means to feed
                and clothe themselves – talents, education,
                all the things the poorest kids in our nation
                have been so wanting.

TARTUFFE   Charles, you've struck me dumb.
                A gift of so magnificent a sum –

CHARLES   Don't speak. No words, the gift is for the cause.
                [Phoning] I'll call my lawyer, Frank at Hawse & Hawse,
                get this done right now. *[Dialling]* If this puts the skids
                under my relations with my own two kids,
                if that's the price I pay – no, no thanks,
                Tartuffe, this has to be the way. Ah, Frank –

        The sound of Mel & Dan singing again as CHARLES begins to exit

                it's Charles. Trust you're well, old chap? Look, I need
                a speedy bit of legal footwork. A deed
                of gift. I'm giving up my Hampstead house,
                donating it in fact. Oh, not a shred of doubt,
                never been more sure of anything in my life ...

        and CHARLES has gone. TARTUFFE pockets the Glen Ord and follows.

ACT FOUR   6.00

The sound of MEL & DAN singing ...

CHILDREN'S HOUR

Pass the Parcel, what's inside?

I am five. I walk on air,
my mother's arms are open wide.
She dances, and I do not hear
– above the lawn, before the rain –
the pellet hit the bouncy castle.
Looking back now I recall
my mother calling as I fall
and the broken metatarsal.

The music's starting up again,
Pass the Parcel ...

The bottle of Glen Ord has been renewed, and the piano cover replaced
TARTUFFE enters and tinkers unmusically on the piano
Enter CLEM, studying a smartphone

CLEM   A good day's work. Social media's gone berserk.
                "Top MP tells Posh Boy son to sling his hook".
                Jesus wept, I can hardly bear to look.
                Danuta called me about this last bizarre
                manoeuvre you've contrived. Just how far
                into madness Charles will dive, God knows!

TARTUFFE   Is it the difficult questions I pose
                just by being here amongst you? It's sad
                when you think about it. You've all had
                advantages other people dream of –
                privilege, ease, enveloped in love –
                and someone comes along without a thing,
                suddenly the carefully structured scaffolding
                begins to totter. Or is it that you act
                like this because you cannot face one fact?

CLEM   What fact?

TARTUFFE   *[Embracing CLEM]* That I love you all unconditionally.
                If you reviled me, turned me from your door,

then I think I'd only love you more.
Dear Clem, is that so hard to comprehend?

CLEM In that case let me address you as a friend.
I admit, until just now, you've played
your cards with consummate skill. You've had it made.
You found your niche, and how you've filled it!
Three square meals per diem, cosy billet,
Charles on hand to pour the single malt –
how could you possibly complain, find fault?
But now, it seems, you'll make him *give this house*
to 'Aspiration U.K.', God knows how.
Oh yes, 'Charitable status pending'
is the line you push. Is there an ending
to that story, or is it just a cover
good for a month or two to plunder
a few good hearts and deep pockets before
your crazy bullshit hits the fan, your paw's
detected in the treacle, as it were?
When the paperwork arrives you'd better stir
it in the embers in the Aga
in the kitchen, bring this tawdry saga
to a close. And as for – God! – make a pass
at my sister, Em? She's out of your class,
as is Mel. How did you dare go there?

TARTUFFE I see. Without a silver spoon I can't go near
these well bred women? Well, I feel no shame.
When we are naked, aren't we all the same?
You disappoint me. I thought you were too big
for prejudice.

CLEM You really are a prig.
I warn you, take your nose from Charles's trough,
quit while you're ahead and quietly bugger off.
Don't wait, go now, before it's way too late.

TARTUFFE I'm going, Clem. Upstairs to meditate.
Why not try it? Can't do any harm,
and, frankly, you do need to be more calm.
It'd bring you peace and show you what is true.

	Here, let me give you another hug.
CLEM	I'd rather not. You're already far too smug. Your performance as an idiot savant is an Oscar winner. But what is it you *really* want? I'd love to know.
TARTUFFE	Ah Clem, I've come to treasure your friendship. It's always such a pleasure to hear you speak. I know that you're a seeker after truth. But sadly that Eureka moment does elude you every time. I have to say, I find it quite sublime.

TARTUFFE exits, passing DANUTA

CLEM	Fucking hell!
DANUTA	Talk with Barrett not go well? He look pleased as Piccadilly swell, I think.
CLEM	Barrett?
DANUTA	Dirk Bogarde in the flick.
CLEM	Oh, I see. He made me look a dick if you must know.

Enter EMMA and MELISSA

EMMA	Clem, thank God you've come! Charles has plans to give away our home! Things are getting out of control.
CLEM	Don't explain. I'm up to speed, I've recced the terrain. Here's my guide – my mole inside the house.
DANUTA	I phone him up. I tell him all things the louse Tartuffe is doing here. How he trick, he swindle. We don't do something quick I scared for Mel that Charlie and that man they wear her down. No longer she have Dan to keep her spirits high.
CLEM	I don't mean to pry

but why on that point conspire to grovel
before Charles? Is this a Victorian novel
we're all caught up in? Marry whom you like.
Tell Tartuffe "get stuffed, go take a hike".
That's easy. It's really not an issue.

MELISSA   *[Tearful]* Danuta, have you got a tissue?
I've something in my eye, and I've got a cold.
Anyway I suppose you must be told,
it's old news now. We've parted. End of chapter.

CLEM   Who, Mel? You and Charles – I mean, your Dad?

MELISSA   No – Val, Val! He's gone, he's packed his bags.

EMMA   Oh, Mel –

MELISSA   So, I'm over twenty-one,
free and single. I deserve some fun
somehow, don't I, for once before I die?

CLEM   Fun seems to be in rather short supply.

MELISSA   Tartuffe's a creep but not an entire disaster.

DANUTA   You crazy. *[To Emma]* Talk to her some sense.

MELISSA   I don't think so. I'm done with the pretence
of love and happy-ever-after.
He's rich, or will be when the royalties roll in.
The way I see it, marrying him is a win-win
situation. His money I'll spend like water
and give him hell. Like a dutiful daughter
I'll please my Dad. And of course I'll cheat
on the sod with every bloke I meet.

CLEM   That's very wise. What a very good idea!
I'm glad to see you've brains between your ears.

EMMA   Clem!

CLEM   No, Tartuffe's a prize. He's certain to be wealthy,
and Mel will need a bank account that's healthy.
I'll call him, shall I?

MELISSA bursts into tears

MELISSA	Don't! … Just let me die.
CLEM	Another tissue, Danuta, dry her eye.
EMMA	It's all right, dearest, your wicked step mum's here.

Enter CHARLES

CHARLES	Oh, all together here? Hello, Clem,
	back now to form a cabal to condemn
	Tartuffe? Does his goodness and simplicity
	offend you so much? Or is it an attack on me?
	Well, I'm used to that. I can't deny
	I have my faults. *[To Melissa]* Expect you wonder why
	my care for you is so often fraught
	with difficulty. I always thought
	'Can't paternal love alone suffice?'
	But you and Dan have had to pay the price
	of losing your Mama at that early age.
	To tell the truth I found it hard to gauge
	the effect on you, became overprotective
	to you both. And then as a corrective
	gave you freedom every way I could.
	In my heart I know how you and Dan would
	have chosen another, simpler life –

MELISSA	Oh Dad!
CHARLES	Thank you, darling – as would my wife.
	If no one minds too much I'll just sit
	and enjoy my family for a bit.
	So carry on. I won't be in the way.

CHARLES sits. No-one knows where to start

EMMA	Charles, you … look, you've had an awful day,
	Why not have a drink? It might cheer
	you up.
CHARLES	I'm absolutely fine. No thanks, dear.
	Clem, *[pointing]* another bottle of that special scotch.
	Please, don't hold back. I'll just sit and watch
	you enjoy yourselves. Just carry on as normal.
CLEM	In that case, if we're being so informal

I think a bracer is exactly what I need.
Anyone else?

CHARLES   Help yourselves. I concede
if I've a fault, it's this wretched thirst
for doing good. I've put public service first.

EMMA   *[To Clem]* Not for me. – What's that you're saying?

CHARLES   Nothing, Emma. Just pondering, weighing
up our situation, thinking aloud.
Looking back, if there's one thing's made me proud
it's knowing Tartuffe and helping him,
watching his name become a synonym
for moral strength and self-reliance.
I've grown so much since our alliance.
Knowing him has so helped me to grasp
how people struggle while their dearest asp-
irations are kicked into the long grass
by the privileged political class.
How different he is from your ex-fiancé,
Mel. That vacuous chancer, happy to betray
your trust –

MELISSA   Please, Dad, just don't –

CLEM   You've got no proof
of that.

CHARLES   Tartuffe –
Tartuffe told us, and Tartuffe wouldn't lie.
Stop it, Mel, I hate to see you cry.
Here's a napkin. Take it, dry your eyes.
There. You know it wouldn't be a surprise
if you didn't find a new happiness
with someone, how shall I say it, less
self-obsessed than Val? Please don't look bereft.
You need a partner with some moral heft,
some inner might. It is my dearest wish
that –

MELISSA   Don't say it!

EMMA   Charles, please …

CHARLES   What? I hate to see her languish
                like this. *[To Mel]* Don't you think that you would feel
                better to acknowledge Tartuffe's appeal?
                I believe it is his moral strength
                itself that makes you nervous, and at length
                you will admit your love. These things run deep.

CLEM   Jesus wept!

MELISSA   Dad, I think the man's a creep!
                I wouldn't marry him or share his bed
                if every other man on earth were dead!

CHARLES   Such vehemence is really quite revealing,
                and indicates the opposite feeling
                to what you say. One makes a show
                of antagonism, when one does not know,
                or won't admit, the power of attraction
                that one feels. It's a common reaction
                and will soon pass.

DANUTA   Nie! She say what she mean!
                If you listen, I'd like to spill the bean,
                tell you all about that total waste of space.

CHARLES   You can go back to Poland, if that's the case.

DANUTA   I no go back. Here I much more happier.
                Your politics crap, Poland's much crappier.
                Law and Justice not giving us our voice.
                They bad as You Know Who.

CHARLES   It's your choice.
                As things stand now I'm perfectly prepared
                to sack you.

DANUTA   Sack me? Ha, that make me scared?
                You going weird. You want make a fight
                I go to Strasbourg, Court of Human Rights.

CHARLES   Oh no, that ship has sailed, I'm glad to say.

DANUTA	Not yet, it haven't. And by the way, I think I go on strike.
CHARLES	Do what you like. But the final decision will be mine.
DANUTA	No. I decide. Is better I resign. I give my cards, effective from today.
CHARLES	Skip all that, just pack your bags. Four weeks' pay will be enough. I've been much too soft, done my best while all of you have scoffed so cynically. I'll be master in my house. No more Mr. Nice Guy. I wear the trousers, don't forget. Melissa, I insist you choose the only man –
MELISSA	Dad!
EMMA	Charles –
CHARLES	– the only man who's got the power to secure your happiness. There is only one union that I could bless, so make your mind up and choose Tartuffe, or never, ever live beneath my roof. Is that clear?

MELISSA suddenly goes to the piano

MELISSA	OK, I'll do it. I don't care. You want a creep to screw your daughter. Fair enough. Just name the day!

She starts to play a tragically sombre Wedding March

EMMA	Charles – Mel, don't play, please! – Charles, this is now beyond a joke. You cannot seriously invoke paternal rights in twenty seventeen. What world is it you inhabit here? How can you contemplate, how dare you even dream of forcing Mel to wed Tartuffe, a man who's scored a constant zed with us on every measure you could think of?

CHARLES   Oh, you pretend, you say that, yes, link up
                 arms to defend that heartless trainee
                 lawyer, Val, who's battened like a leech
                 on Mel. Well, thank God, she's ditched him now,
                 which leaves her free and clear again to plough
                 a richer furrow. This is my honest attempt
                 to make a better life for her, exempt
                 from all the meaningless distraction
                 of London life. And the satisfaction
                 of joining me in helping make a change.

CLEM   With Tartuffe? I'm sorry, you're deranged.
                 I don't intend to just sit back and watch
                 while you make the most colossal botch
                 of your career, your family, and your life.
                 You choose to trust Tartuffe and not your wife?
                 You've been sold a pup, you're way beyond naïve,
                 it appears you actually believe
                 this aspiration crap Tartuffe is selling.
                 What is it that you find so compelling?

CHARLES   I refuse to indulge your sneering anymore.

CLEM   You used to be a political herbivore,
                 level-headed, hardworking, dedicated
                 to the job. In the past I'd always rated
                 you as a grownup, despite our different views.
                 Have you lost your nerve or just blown a fuse?
                 You've swallowed the whole bag of tricks,
                 the newest convert to post-truth politics.
                 'Cut benefits', that's the way to help the poor,
                 with one of them on hand to assure
                 you of the right of what you're doing.
                 That's not policy, it's magical thinking,
                 and all the time the Ogden ship is sinking.

CHARLES   You were always left wing, doctrinaire,
                 a political lightweight, Clem. Not a prayer
                 of making real change. Why don't you hop it?

MELISSA   Dad, please –

DANUTA   Do cholery!

CLEM   Charles, please stop it!

EMMA   That's enough, all of you! Not another word!
                Charles, I will not tolerate this absurd
                behaviour a single minute more.
                This plan to *give away our house*, and poor
                Mel – it's as insulting as it is deranged!
                I've decided what to do – arrange
                a test, if you like a little *opéra bouffe*.
                Only two of us required on stage. Tartuffe
                and I will act while *[to Charles]* you remain unseen
                and be a silent referee between
                turpitude and truth. Play your part,
                Charles, in this or I'll eject you smartly
                from this house, together with that misfit
                boyfriend, God – however Tartuffe sits
                in your deluded mind. No talk of headlines
                please, I couldn't care a damn, all fine
                by me if you're caught pressing on the bell,
                begging to be let back in. Clem and Mel,
                the kitchen.

CHARLES   What – ?

EMMA   *[To Clem & Mel]* Now, please!
                                              CLEM & MEL exit
                Now, Danuta,
                you to Tartuffe, say I have a mind ... to tutor
                him on the piano. Say I'm a little sad.
                You could imply ... no, you might just add
                that Charles is out and won't be back till late.

DANUTA   This sound good plan. Your wife she playing bait.
                A honey trap for creepy bottom pain
                Tartuffe.

EMMA   Danuta, go!
                                              DANUTA exits
                May I be plain?
                If you don't play ball in this –

CHARLES	In what? In what?
EMMA	If you don't play ball in this, our knot's untied, our marriage ends, like Monty Python's parrot dead, kaput, it's gone, an ex-marriage, Charles, do I make that clear?
CHARLES	I'm reeling, I'm confused, please, Emma dear – !
EMMA	Listen, won't you? Seeing is believing! And it's the only way to stop me leaving – no scratch that, I'm going anyway, I don't think I could stick another day in this poisonous atmosphere – but I think it's time you were made aware of what's been happening. Under the piano. Quick!
CHARLES	The piano?
EMMA	Under the piano. The only way you'll know the truth from self-deluding fantasy. Well, 'husband-dear', what's it going to be?
CHARLES	I – well – I – oh, very well, I'll hide.

> *CHARLES crawls under the piano*
> *EMMA starts to play Chopin's E Minor Prelude*
> *CHARLES re-emerges*

	Really, Em, this is so undignified.

> *Enter DANUTA*

DANUTA	He come!

> *Exit DANUTA*

CHARLES	Oh God!

> *He crawls back under the piano*
> *EMMA resumes playing*
> *Enter TARTUFFE*

TARTUFFE	Emma, you wanted me, so now I'm here.
EMMA	Like a drink? Scotch, or we could have a beer?
TARTUFFE	Thank you, no, not now. Am I to deduce that tutoring is simply an excuse? Has your brother set you to try to rein

	back on Charles' munificence – retain your home, your privileged London dwelling?
EMMA	What? Oh no, please understand that, well, this house belongs to Charles, and Dan and Mel. Like you, I've been an interloper here and to be frank, it reeks – the atmosphere – just a little too much of Ogdens past – and present. I'll be out of here so fast Charles will have to run to keep up. No, do I need a reason to want some company?
TARTUFFE	I sense your spirit needs some calming. The vibrations in this house are harming your inner peace. Try and focus in, then you may find our spirits are akin, aligned to meet on a higher plain.

He makes to leave

EMMA	No, don't go. Don't leave me on my own again. And why go back to being moralistic just when we've solved the logistic problem of how be alone?
TARTUFFE	What?
EMMA	Or do you feel the need to atone for getting caught – your last indiscretion? I understand if you've learned your lesson. But it's as you said. Charles is no great shakes in bed, quite the opposite. It takes hours of tedious foreplay. Then when I'm hot, before you know it, he's gone and shot the lot in less than a nano-second.
TARTUFFE	I reckoned as much. You being straight? What's changed?
EMMA	Everything. No need for us to dance around now. We may never get a chance like this again. Dan isn't here to butt in, you've seen to that. Charles is busy, shut in by a three-line whip. It's just us two,

so, 'Tartuffe', aren't you going to do
something about it?

TARTUFFE   I think I'd rather sit
upstairs and read a book.
Tell me, do you really think I look
like an idiot? I reckon it's a con.
Maybe you think if you can turn me on
you'll soften me up. Is that what this is
all in aid of? That really pisses
me off. Don't fanny me about.

EMMA   Goodness me! It's quite uncanny
to watch your personality switching.
I have to say I find it quite bewitching.
There's 'our kid', still bleeding
from his trauma, damaged but altogether caring
and inspiring. Then the business guru,
the new-age kind, a delicious brew
of mystic mantras and – I'd take a bet –
cut-throat practice, tease and threat?
Then the "Let's get to it, darlin" macho
guy who knows no girl could tell him 'no'.
But now this last persona –
the suspicious, enigmatic loner,
keeping the lid on his rebellious id.
Tell me, who's the real you, our kid?

TARTUFFE   Depends. Which d'you like the best?

EMMA   Oh, the macho is the sexiest
by far, not the last bit, or the new age stuff.
I prefer you as a bit of rough.

TARTUFFE   You like your oyster with a bit of grit,
you dirty girl?

EMMA   Now, that's more like it.
Plain speaking turns me on.
I began to think the real man had gone.

TARTUFFE   My god, you are being straight. Never reckoned

	you would make the first move.
EMMA	What does it take for me to prove that you're in luck?
TARTUFFE	Fucking hell, you've changed your tune. I love it. You can tell old Charles that he can shove it where the sun don't shine.
EMMA	Why do you keep staring at my neckline? Like a little boy ogling at a sweetshop window.
TARTUFE	You saying you want me to stop or what?
EMMA	That's not what I mean.
TARTUFFE	When you're a kid like I was, and times are lean you dream of the sweets your parents don't allow – pear drops, licorice, yielding marshmallow –

He pulls at the neckline of EMMA'S frock

	ooh, lovely stuff. I often think about you in the buff, with your kit off, all pink and rosy.
EMMA	That all sounds very cosy. You know how to sweep me off my feet.
TARTUFFE	*[Undoing his belt]* It's not hard. I reckon you're on heat.
EMMA	Oh that is so perfectly romantic! Wait – Tartuffe, darling, not so frantic –
TARTUFFE	Look, the rough you wanted needs a shag. Come on, Em, you want it, like a slag!

A groan from CHARLES which Emma disguises as her own

EMMA	Arrrgh! … But not so quick, you scallywag! Let's take our time. It must never be a rush.
TARTUFFE	I don't have time to beat about the bush!

Unseen by Tartuffe, CHARLES emerges from under the piano

EMMA   But a Hap Chi master never jumps the gun.
                You know – anticipation's half the fun!
                You need to cool your ardour just a bit.
                Why not go and mix us both a gin and it?
                Then we'll put our heads together, invent
                the right scenario, something truly decadent.

TARTUFFE   Lovely stuff. I like a bit of strange.

EMMA   Quickly now, go and arrange
                those drinks.
                                                    TARTUFFE goes out
                Mine with heaps and heaps of ice!

TARTUFFE   *[Off]* Tell you what I think might be nice …

EMMA   What's that? *[To Charles]* Get back! So much more to see
                and hear.

TARTUFFE   *[Off]* I've always had this little fantasy –

CHARLES   More than I can bear.

TARTUFFE   *[Off]* Em? You all right in there?

        EMMA pushes CHARLES down as TARTUFFE looks in, holding a cocktail
                                                                    shaker
EMMA   Yes, fine!

TARTUFFE   *[As he goes out again]* About this little fantasy of mine …
                What about a threesome? You know –

EMMA   What?

TARTUFFE   *[Off]* I've always fancied giving it a go.
                You, me and maybe tight-arsed Mel.

                                            CHARLES pops up again
                We might even get Danuta in as well,
                the more the merrier. What about it?

EMMA   Your personal harem. I doubt it
                would go down well with Mel's dad.

                            She pushes Charles down again as
            TARTUFFE enters with two glasses of gin & it and a packet of nuts

TARTUFFE	What, Charles? I don't see how it's that sad old tosser's business. He can stuff himself for all I care. I've had enough. I've outgrown him. I just don't need him. Why should I have to feed him all that new age crap? Not necessary. Here you go. You want to know the cherry on the cake?
EMMA	You're like the cat that's got the cream.
TARTUFFE	Listen, darling, in your wildest dream you wouldn't guess how much cream I've got. Chin Chin!
EMMA	How much?
TARTUFFE	What?
EMMA	Cream?
TARTUFFE	I've got the lot. Your hubby's no more use to me, Em, I'm going to cut him loose. The thing is, I've got a charity to run, and he's a risk. Pity, but there you go. Cashew?
EMMA	I think you'll find that Charles will sue.
TARTUFFE	More likely he'll be selling the Big Issue outside Aldi in the rain. He hasn't got the guts or resources. We've got him by the nuts. When it gets out, he'll resign his seat. You know, I reckon I could easily beat that Corbyn mob. I'll stand in Charles's place. [Taking her glass] Talking of which, I feel the pace is getting quicker here. Forget the foursome, and the floor is fine …
EMMA	Oh, no – !
TARTUFFE	[Dropping his trousers] Oh yes, yes, on your bum, quick, Emma! God, I'm going to come!

| EMMA | What? But you can keep it up for hours, can't you? Those fantastic Tantric powers? |

EMMA   What? But you can keep it up for hours,
         can't you? Those fantastic Tantric powers?

TARTUFFE Our Kid wants his sweeties now!

A crash from under the piano

CHARLES   Owwww!!!

EMMA   Charles?

TARTUFFE You lying cow!

EMMA   Get a doctor, he may be concussed.

TARTUFFE Quiet! Your ministrations will only disgust
          poor Charles, after what he's overheard.

EMMA   What?

TARTUFFE Leave this to me. Not another word.

EMMA   But –

TARTUFFE Charles, if you can hear me, just nod ...
          He's OK, he's fine, he'll live, thank God.
          Charles, dear friend, there are things I must explain,
          some of which I fear will cause you pain.
          Please nod your head if you can follow ...

Apparently CHARLES nods again

          I know that it's a bitter pill to swallow.
          It started with good intentions. Your dear Emma
          insisted she help me resolve the dilemma
          of the cruel memories buried in my past –

EMMA   Dear God!

TARTUFFE – my mother's profession, which cast
          a shadow, blasting every day.
          Emma suggested a form of role-play.
          She'd be my mother, while I would be a punter.
          In this way I would confront her
          malign influence on my life head-on.
          And it's worked. My trauma's gone.
          If it had stayed like that, it would all be fine,
          but somewhere, she strayed across a line

that separates play-acting from desire.
All at once it seemed as if a fire
consumed her. She threw off all restraint,
begged me to take her. God knows I'm not a saint,
but I fought back, to save you both from shame.
Perhaps in some way, it's me that is to blame.
Yes, I must be the guilty one. Why? Because
I could not see how vulnerable she was.
She's in need of help, that's the truth of it.
Charles?

A silence

CHARLES   You absolute, copper-bottomed shit.

He emerges from under the piano, holding the back of his head

You hypocrite, you vile disgusting louse.
Defame my wife? Get out of my house.
Don't bother to pack. Wait! No,
I'm going to kill you before you go.

EMMA   Darling, sit down. There must be some other /
way –

TARTUFFE   Look at him. I don't know why I bother.
Threatening me, when he's the busted flush.
I'm the one who's giving him the push.
His posh brief Frank didn't hang about.
Signed and sealed. Here, read the printout.
There's nothing anyone can do to stop me.
I'll be generous, Em, I know you tried to drop me
in it, but you can stay on if you'd like?

EMMA   Ha!

TARTUFFE   Then both of you get on your bike
and disappear. I'm better off without you.
I've got things to tell the tabloids about you.
Now bugger off. I'm going up to sleep.
You needn't pack, there's nothing you can keep.

TARTUFFE exits
EMMA thrusts the printout to Charles and exits
The lights fade on Charles, as Mel & Dan sing again.

ACT FIVE   8.00

CHARLES & CLEM. CHARLES holds a bag of frozen peas to his head

CHARLES   It's historically determined, Clem.
           The Revolution's come, our kind's condemned
           to the guillotine. Tartuffe's my Robespierre.
           Obscene but true. There's nothing just or fair.
           Em hates me now. Who could possibly blame
           her? My idiocy's pitched us into shame
           and ignominy.

CLEM   But why in heaven's name
           befriend a pot of poison like Tartuffe?

CHARLES   I'm bemused myself, if you want the truth.
           I'd found myself adrift, I'd forgot
           the whys and wherefores, on autopilot
           I suppose, then brought up short by your 'pot
           of poison'. Lived through terrible events,
           abused by his parents, yet reinvents
           himself, makes a packet in the East,
           and with it a truth intriguingly off piste
           for a conventional chap like me. Revelation
           at last, blueprint for national salvation.
           'Aspiration UK', designed to educate
           every individual to be master of his fate.

CLEM   How on earth did he get the dosh,
           spouting this crypto-fascist tosh?
           God, Charles, you've been royally had.

CHARLES   Don't, Clem. I think I've been a little mad.
           More than a little, actually.

CLEM   I just don't see
           why your colleagues didn't smell a rat.

CHARLES   You'd be surprised. It wasn't quite like that.
           Many thought it was a jolly good idea.

CLEM   That figures. So where do you go from here?

CHARLES   I've had it with populism. 'Ordinary decent folk'

are just a whining, deeply unfunny joke
without a punch line. And in wretched taste,
I see that now. I've no more time to waste
on the masses and the feculent dross
that we're told is their 'honest patriotism'.
It's racism. And as for their abysmal
opinions on culture – "Game shows are a lot
more use than opera" – no, they're not!
"Soap operas more relevant than Shakespeare"?
No! What's left to us now but to sneer
at the lot of them?

CLEM   You lurch between extremes.
                One minute you endorse Tartuffe's mad schemes
                to exalt the common man, then you switch.
                Suddenly, like Shakespeare's Timon, you ditch
                every semblance of rational good sense,
                revile the human race and dispense
                your bile quite indiscriminately.

CHARLES   I take it you don't agree with me.

CLEM   No, I don't. Your's is not just an elitist view,
                it's semi-fascist and I'm shocked that you
                endorse it. To be a politician to any degree
                you must have at least some touch of empathy
                with the folk that freely give their vote.
                                              Enter DANIEL

CHARLES   I know, I know. But now that the lifeboat
                is sinking, I want a final shout.

DANIEL   Dad –

CHARLES   My God, Daniel –

DANIEL   Before you throw me out
                again, tell me what's going on. I came to say
                I've got a job, a part to really play
                at last, but out there there's Em and Mel in tears.

CHARLES   Of course they are. You won't believe your ears,
                I've been insane. Your future – you and Mel –

I've lost the lot. Your idiot father fell
into the web of that odious lout,
Tartuffe –

Enter PAMELA & DANUTA

PAMELA   Charles, what is this all about?
Emma called me. Some crisis couldn't wait?

CHARLES   Indeed it can't. I can't believe our fate.
It's not a crisis, it's a cataclysm.
We have fallen, crashed into an abysm.
That man Tartuffe, has robbed us of our home!
And not content with that – it makes me foam
to think it – declared the deepest love for Mel
when all the time he really craved a spell
or two of kinky sex with Em! Seduce
my wife, after all ... oh, what's the use?
I'm finished. I can't believe we've been
so stupid, you and I. Can't we have seen,
how could we fail? Our brains on hold, or what?

PAMELA   Charles, stop at once. You really do talk rot
at times. There's been some ludicrous mistake,
of course. I'm not surprised. It would take
something really beyond the pale here –
Daniel joining Isis or *Emma* turning queer –
to make me blink at any new kind
of carry-on.

Enter EMMA, followed by MELISSA

EMMA   Pam –

CHARLES   Mother, please! D'you think I'm blind?
I saw Tartuffe try to have Em on the floor.
After he'd proposed a threesome, or a four
with Melissa and Danuta too.

DANUTA   Gowno!

PAMELA   You *thought* you saw. You *thought* you heard a few
quite innocent blandishments. Emma is
a woman who works quite hard to draw this
sort of male attention.

EMMA gasps

Even as a child
you jumped too quickly to such grossly wild
conclusions.

CHARLES   The only thing that's wild or gross
is that worm Tartuffe and his grandiose
plot to rob me of daughter, wife and home.
Should I have taken pictures on my phone,
shown him ogling Emma's cleavage, groping
sweaty fingers up her thighs / or – ?

PAMELA   Charles, you're getting
smutty! You're not a boy of twelve, please rein
in these adolescent fictions. It's plain
that something Tartuffe's said – misheard I'm sure –
has discovered in you a vein of pure
hysteria. I've noticed it before.

CHARLES   Something's he's said? I've misheard? I saw
it with these eyes! Is there a piano here,
in this room? I think there is, or is it fear
of shiny black things makes me fantasise?

PAMELA   Now you're being silly. I ask you to be wise,
calm down and recognise that in this pit
of prejudice against Tartuffe things have hit
another low. Innuendo, slander, class
bias, they've all contrived an imagined farce
worthy of Feydeau – no, of Brian Rix.

CHARLES   Christ, mother, can't you lose this *idée fixe*
about Tartuffe?

DANUTA   No. She deaf to 'this is tricks'
no more than you. We tell you 'conman', 'fraud',
you say not so. Blindness I see is flaw
in Ogden genes.

PAMELA   That's quite enough from you.
You're the font of all this ballyhoo,
spreading slander everywhere you please –

Tartuffe, my dearest friend Claire Frost. Easy
to be smart, much harder to conceal
you're Polish, you cannot know how it feels
to be diminished by the English class divide.

DANUTA   Maybe feels like being Polish. I'd side
with 'our kid' *[snapping fingers]* like that if he not scumbag
only you and Charlie here let drag
you into madness.

Charles' mobile has begun to ring – 'The Ride of the Valkyries'

PAMELA   What insolence – !
Oh, for God's sake take the call, it might be sense
that's someone's talking. Here's all offensive
fantasy and lies.

CHARLES   Hullo – oh God, it's Number Ten! ...
Prime Minister, splendid, I wondered when –
Sorry? Yes, of course ... *[squeaky tirade]*... Yes, yes, I see.
Well, some questions do ... *[a bit more]* ... admittedly –
Prime Minister? Er, hello? – She's hung up.

EMMA   What is it, Charles?

MELISSA   Dad, what's happened?

CLEM   What's up?

CHARLES   Says she's just misspent two precious hours of life
reading 'Our Kid'. Made her want to take a knife
and slit her throat. So grotesquely maudlin,
she said, she couldn't possibly consider in
her cabinet anyone who'd give it time of day.

CLEM   No promotion then?

CHARLES   Worse. I'm sacked. Conway
Grout has got my job. I'm out. Back with
all those Brexiteers, with Jones and Smith,
and all those oiks infest the upper tiers
and shout 'hyar hyar', and shed a tear
when Maggie's ghost's invoked. If Tartuffe's game
hadn't been the scam from hell my name

at Number Ten would still be marked in red.

He collapses on the sofa. The doorbell rings. Nobody moves

DANUTA   The door. It ring. I answer it, or let
                  man or girl what calls grow old on step?

EMMA   Please, Danuta.

                                                    DANUTA exits

PAMELA   I really thought Theresa
                  had the sense, the acumen to seize a
                  book like 'Our Kid' and penetrate to its
                  profounder meanings, underneath the fits
                  of rage, the occasional lapse of tone
                  to which, I admit, our dear Tartuffe is prone.

CHARLES   'Dear Tartuffe'! I could kill you, mother!

*Enter DANUTA with DES LOYAL. At various moments DES records his
                                      'copy' on a dictaphone*

DES   Whoops, have I happened on a spot of bother?
                  Evening, Ladies.

CLEM   Des, you old bugger!

DES   Clem!

CLEM   Who'd have thought
                  we'd be graced by the legendary dreadnought
                  of the 'Sunday Shocker'? How's it going?

DES   Been better. The old Sigmunds are doing
                  me in. I can't sit down.

CLEM   Shame. And Mrs. Des?

DES   Bit peaky, too, you could say, just at pres.
                  Been royally conned, some bastard on the phone
                  sold her a time-share at Estepona
                  that wasn't even built. That was last year,
                  but she's still upset. No sun and sangria.

CLEM   Tut. It's a wicked world. Send her my love.

PAMELA   Who is this man, Charles? Heavens above,
                  he marches in, as if he were royalty.

CLEM	He is. Meet the legend that is Des Loyal, king of the tabloid stings.
CHARLES	Oh God!
PAMELA	I know nothing of his reputation, so go only on his insolence. Why is he here?
DES	Your boy, Tartuffe, he wants to bend my ear. *[To Charles]* He's going to stitch you up like a kipper.
PAMELA	I beg your pardon?
DES	Granted, dear. Stick a story on you will run a month or more. Sex games, fun. A little kinky foreplay and then the full Zambezi. Wahay! It's smarmy Ogdens' Nut Brown Flake. I don't even have to dress up as a sheikh to get the scoop of the year, the best story. "Secret vice-romps in home of Top Tory" – that should hit the spot.
CHARLES	What?
EMMA	What?
DANIEL	Hey?
PAMELA	Kippers, rivers, stings, and 'kinky foreplay'? Charles, have you been fantasising again?
DES	Understatement. From fantasy and then to action from what I hear. Compliant cast of wife, daughter, son, and with a blast of Euro-immigrant novelty for luck.
CHARLES	Jesus Christ!
MEL	Dad – !
DANIEL	What the fuck – ?
PAMELA	Quiet, all of you! Danuta, go away!

DANUTA	OK! OK! 'Euro immigrant' obey!

DANUTA exits

PAMELA   Clem, I must say, I don't know how you can
             have become acquainted with this beastly man,
             but could you prevail on him to leave
             before I get a little sharp? I see
             I have to take my family in hand.

CLEM   Pamela, please, let's try to understand?
             Des, old pal, it seems that as a grace note,
             if you like, to the sinking of the Ogden boat
             that he himself's procured, the man 'Tartuffe'
             has told you a farago of untruth
             about their private lives. Would that be fair?

DES   Good story, Clem. Untruth? You've got me there.
             I'm on the fence on that one. At least until
             tomorrow's deadline pricks my bum.

CLEM   Well, look –

CHARLES   Allow me, Clem.
             Mr. Loyal, of course I know you by repute.
             I enjoy, and respect, your tireless pursuit –
             be quiet, mother – of tales to entertain
             a discriminating readership, the pain
             it costs you, particularly as you suffer
             from – well, let's not dwell on that. However,
             as a juster tale with which to regale
             your 'loyal' readers on the sabbath day,
             could I interest you in an infamous attack
             on a public-spirited, thoroughly decent chap,
             hardworking MP, ex-minister of state –

DES   Hold it! That would be you, I take it?

CHARLES   Indeed it would.

DES   Sacked you, has she? Well, I know you're backed
             into a corner, but no can do.
             Like I said I'm seeing Tartuffe. He's due
             for an exclusive interview. Quite a tale to tell:

"Our kid sex slave in MP's house of hell",
that's how we're going to play it.

PAMELA   You disgusting man, get out!

                              TARTUFFE has entered in bare feet
DES   I think not.

TARTUFFE   You must be Des. *[Shaking hands]* Delighted. Ogdens, what,
              still here? *And* the OAP! You've got some nerve,
              I'll give you that. A bunch of Tory perves
              sitting here like Lord and Lady Muck?
              You pollute this gracious suburb. Go suck
              on someone else's hospitality. Here
              you're through.

PAMELA   Tartuffe … !

TARTUFFE   Not shocked, I hope, old dear?
              The Ogden mask has fallen. Surely you
              were wise to what the four of them get up to?

PAMELA   I can't imagine what you … Tartuffe, I … I …

TARTUFFE   Dame P. struck dumb! Can't even say 'bye-bye'?
              Shall we retire to my office, Des? Upstairs?
              Leave the low life to sling their hooks? It tears
              your heart to see them squirm.

                              He turns to EMMA with an open letter
              Almost forgot –
              this came for you yesterday. Seems the docs
              have got the results of all those tests you took.
              Say 'please, Tartuffe' and I'll let you have a look.
              Oh no, no, no, not so quick.
              Technically, I should post it on, stick
              it in the box outside, re-addressed to Shelter,
              Camden Town – "I do so hope you find her".

                              EMMA snatches it from him
CHARLES   Em, what is it, dear?

MEL   What's it say?

                  EMMA scans the letter, then presses it to her face

EMMA	I'm clear. The scan, it – it doesn't show a tumour.
CHAR & MEL	Thank God!

EMMA and CHARLES embrace

TARTUFFE	Ah, how sweet! Shame about the rumour from number 10. His boss, Theresa's blown a fuse. Should have heard her rant, the way she abused you. "You've lost the plot, Charles, you're on your own!"
CHARLES	You've read Em's mail – and tapped my phone?
TARTUFFE	Nice story, Des. Mind, she talked a lot of guff about my book. She doesn't know her stuff.
DANIEL	That's enough. I'm not going to stand aside while you abuse my family, you snake-eyed bastard!
TARTUFFE	Grown a pair of bollocks, Dan? Come on then, if you think you're nearly man enough!

DANIEL decks him

You can't do that. I'll have the law on you!
You little shit, you could have killed me.

*The other members of the cast stop and watch as DES addresses his
Sunday Shocker audience*

DES	"Top Tory linked to violent spree! Disgraced minister, Charles Ogden, sixty-three –
CHARLES	I'm fifty-four –
DES	– watched as gay 'actor' son, Danny, twenty-four –"
DANIEL	It's Daniel – and I'm twenty-three.
DES	"Twenty-three – left bleeding on the floor celebrity abuse victim, Tartuffe, AKA 'Our Kid', in a frenzied, wild affray –" I don't think this one is a runner, 'Tuffe.
TARTUFFE	What? You're a witness. You've got the proof, write it down.

DES	No, won't sell. Handbags at dawn? Frankly no one cares, it's just a yawn. What your reader wants is titillation, not some bit of soppy aggravation. My meter's running, time to spill the beans about all those kinky sex scenes you promised me. I've pressed record, so fire away, old son.
TARTUFFE	Just need time to realign my chakras. Des, your readers cannot know what I've been through. It's – it's all a show. Respectable? No, they're all sex mad, the lot of 'em. The public's been had by their hypocrisy.
MEL	Hypoc – that's rich!
TARTUFFE	Of course, she'll deny it. Randy bitch!
DES	*Sexual* hypocrisy, I take it?
CLEM	Des, my dear chap, you can't begin to credit –
TARTUFFE	They can't fake it anymore. The whole house is obsessed with sex. Anything could arouse their perverted desires.
PAMELA	Outrageous!
CLEM	The man's a world-class liar.
TARTUFFE	The Right Hon Charlie Ogden likes to watch, under the piano, while Emma makes some botch'd, pathetic attempt to get my trousers off.
DES	"In Leafy Hampstead, Sex Mad Tory Toff, Peeping Ogden, Begs 'Our Kid' On The Sly To Perform With His Missus, So He Can Spy On Sizzling Toy Boy Sex. Said curvaceous Emma, thirty four – "
EMMA	I'm forty-one.
DES	" – thirty-four,

twenty-two, thirty-four, my hubby loves it best
when some tanned and hunky house guest
gives me a seeing-to on the yoga mat,
while he – "

EMMA   What? I never said anything like that.

DES   Quiet, love, you'll interrupt my flow.

                                    DANUTA has entered unnoticed

DANUTA   Stop!

DES   Pardon?

DANUTA   Is time somebody tell you 'No,
                this not news'. It making me annoyed,
                is just gloating, is schadenfreude,
                is like to make fun, is prurient.

DES   What I always say is 'bent is bent'.

EMMA   Danuta –

DANUTA   It my turn to talk! Tell much cuter
                story than this man. It true too, which make
                some difference, I think, or is only fake
                things good on front of tabloid paper news?

DES   I wouldn't go that far. You might choose
                the truth when it has some fizz, some sex,
                but she's a dry old bitch most days and the next
                day's copy's due. You Polish, Latvian,
                can't seem to – ?

DANUTA   Listen me, Loyal-man.
                You want true story, I give you one,
                but you shut up good. This fraud, this son
                of bitch with stupid name – he think tartuffe
                a cake! –

EMMA   Danuta,
                I know you mean to help, but are you sure – ?

PAMELA   Emma! Let Danuta speak. In the war
                those Polish airmen brought such steel and flair

I've hopes a perceptive child of theirs
can rescue us again.

DANUTA   1959
my father born. But thank you, Pam. *[At the door]* It time
you come in, now! *[To the others]* Time reveal you know
how peasant cook and banished Romeo –

VAL enters

MEL   Val!

DANUTA   – pull mat from under fraudy feet, and show
some brain what missing here too long.

TARTUFFE   Oh look. You come to hit me too, impress
the angry ex? Or no – just let me guess –
our trainee lawyer thinks he'll raise some
technical dispute to stop the fun?
Dream on. Innit, mon – hey Des, listen to da youf –

DES   Oy, less of that, Tartuffe! Doesn't sound too clever.

TARTUFFE   Whatever. Well, thanks, to me, you've been
too late on this one, Val. Got you off the scene
in time. That pal of Charles' at Hawes & Hawes,
pissed as a fish after a liquid lunch, didn't pause
to think, but got online and wrapped the whole
thing up in minutes. Even the moles
at the land registry say this place is mine.

VAL   *[Producing print-out]* I know. I've got the entry, all the fine
detail too. "By deed of gift, legal title
passed from Ogden, Charles Piers Par ... ?

CHARLES   Parsifal.

VAL   – to Aspiration UK." All tied up like
a turkey at Christmas. But we have to spike
your tyres, Tartuffe. If you grope Danuta
with one hand, sign into your computer
with the other you risk she might catch sight
of what you type. Big mistake. And downright
strange, that password. 'C-h-u-t-i-y-a'.
It had me foxed at first.

CHARLES   Oh I can say
                that. 'Chutiya'. A chant, an ancient Sanskrit word
                Tartuffe taught me.

DANUTA   Sanskrit, no. Chant? Absurd.
                It Hindi. – I take course in Cracow, go
                to India before my *PhD*. –
                In Hindi 'chutiya'. In Polish see
                'ciota' or 'chuju'. In franker
                English translate best, I think, as 'wanker'.

CHARLES   Oh my god, and so ... and what about
                [Chanting] Vahaan ek har minat ka janm? Not devout?

DANUTA   How you say – *[Chanting]* 'There's one born every minute'?

CHARLES   You bastard!

DES   Nice one, 'Tuffe, I like it.

TARTUFFE   Cheers, Des. But shall we cut to the chase?
                You've hacked my system, think you have a case
                to stiff me on the grounds that Aspiration UK
                aint as squeaky clean as Charlie here may
                have thought. You're pissing in the wind, the house
                and all the dosh, it's mine. There's a flash Scouse
                builder on his way to change the locks.
                So pack your knickers, funsters all, your socks
                and anything else that reeks of Ogdens,
                Polish, blacks, dames, gays or hacks and wend
                your merry ways. The rest will go on ebay.

PAMELA   This is monstrous!

EMMA   Now, Mr Loyal, you see the truth, the way
                this man's deceived my husband, you can't pursue
                these libellous claims, these disgusting blue
                movie fictions any further, can you?

                                      DES sucks his teeth

TARTUFFE   Tricky, Des. I can see you're on the spot.
                Page one sex, or "'Our Kid's' autobiog not
                quite kosher", buried on nine or ten?

	I feel for you, old chap.
DES	Thanks, you're a gent. So what's the scam, young man? Aspiration UK a front for Tartuffe's personal doomsday fund?
VAL	Broadly speaking, yes. As far from 'charitable status pending' as tar is from treacle.
TARTUFFE	The treacle's still all mine.
VAL	And as far as 'Our Kid' goes, may I shine a little light? Mr Tapper here – that's his name – wasn't raised by a mother on the game, or a drunken Dad. As for that decrepit caravan in Wales, he's never stepped it north of Luton in his life. A minor public school in Ashford had to sign him out for blackmailing gay teachers. And selling 'matron porn' to the chaplain's son.
TARTUFFE	I was proud of that one, showed a lot of nerve.
VAL	As for making some great pot of money selling mobiles in Nepal – and those schools he built? – no evidence at all. 'Our Kid' is fiction, a tawdry cut-and-paste of sordid, sentimental cliché laced with lies. He didn't even write it. Got some alcoholic hack invent the lot for a case or two of cut price gin.
TARTUFFE	So that's a sin? I say again I've all the treacle. What's a bit of shame when you've a million or three for oxygen?
VAL	D'you think so?
TARTUFFE	I know so, Buster, run along.
VAL	So 'Allcard versus Skinner''s not a song

you know the words to? Or the legal term,
'undue influence'? When a donor's turned
to giving under pressure, or fraudulent
misrepresentation by recipient?

VAL gives TARTUFFE a print-out, which he studies. A pause

CHARLES   Tell me, Clem, what exactly is 'matron porn'?

VAL   Believe me, you really don't want to know.

TARTUFFE   Come upstairs, Charlie, and I'll give you a show.
             Just the thing for a clapped-out old-school Tory.

VAL   It's over, Tapper. If I were you I'd worry.

TARTUFFE   Sorry mate, worrying's for wimps. If Charlie's
             happy to be seen for the stupid sap he is,
             then get your man at Hawes and Hawes to do
             the honours. If you can still afford a blue-
             blooded brief like him, that is. You're broke,
             I'm flush. Fuck Allcard and Skinner, I hold
             all the cards on this one. Come upstairs
             with Mr Tapper, Des? No call me Vic. Share
             a Glen Ord, while I give you the best sex
             story the Sunday Shocker's seen since "ex-
             stripper poos in PM's shoe".

DES   I never drink. 'Vic'?

TARTUFFE   The name with which my genteel parents ticked
             the box.

DES   'Vic Tapper' then?

TARTUFFE   Got it in one,
             old friend of my heart. The loved but errant son
             of Leonard and Ursula. But come, let's –

DES   I'm almost lost for words. If I'd laid bets
             who it was I'd come across ... You're the lower
             form of life that took that honest flower
             of English womanhood, my darling wife,
             and sold her time-share dreams. That's the life,
             you said, a paradise, a corner of a Spanish

field that is forever England. But will vanish
as soon as I can bank the cash. Sun, sangria?
I think you might have added sex for her.
She's sixty-nine, you crafty piece of shit!

TARTUFFE   Des –

DES   That smirk of yours – beginning to make
me wince. I don't know how you dare to shake
the hands of honest folk like these. Con them
out of house and home? I was about to pen
their dreadful tale when you poisoned
us with your noisome presence. Slander
the Right Hon Ogden here, draw him as a pander
in some fictitious sex romp? I don't know
how you have the nerve. This evil won't go
unpunished, I promise that. My austere
organ – circulation in the millions, fearless
advocate of British values, patriotism, truth,
guardian of the morals of shining youth
and trembling age – will take you to the cleaners,
Vic. Anything to say – just between us
and my loyal readers?
                                        Doorbell rings again

VAL   We should perhaps
allow the right of silence? There's the chaps
in blue, I think. *[Referring to Danuta]* We did alert them
to the fraud. And the libellous, *ad hominem*
attack on the Ogdens' private lives.
That time-share scam of his, duping innocent wives,
well, the icing on the cake.

DES   I like your drift
young man. Here's my 'Loyalty' card. Always shift

The doorbell rings again, and knocking. DANUTA exits

for legal brains in my world – oops, times up.
You'll want your shoes. No carpet in the lockup.
                    TARTUFFE bolts through the French windows

MELISSA   Stop him! Stop him!

DAN chases after, while the others go to the window to watch, except
for VAL who exits to the front door

DES	Quite a turn of speed there! "Barefoot fraudster spurns frank interview with men in blue and leaps a privet hedge, fails" – I hope – "to keep well clear of fiercely prickly briar rose – "
TARTUFFE	*[Off]* Arrggh!
DES	– ooh, that's torn it nicely! – "then goes like streak of piss 'cross handsome Lutyens square –

Police siren starts

	Old Bill in hot pursuit!"
PAMELA	Oh, do please spare us!

DAN re-enters from garden and VAL and DANUTA from hall

DANIEL	They wouldn't let me chase the chap!
CLEM	Perhaps they didn't want a murder rap for Des to paint in Sunday Shocker technicolor.
DAN	But I –
CHARLES	Just leave it, Dan, let them do their job. You decked him once, let that be that.
EMMA	Yes, Dan, please. Good riddance. Let him run.
DAN	But –
MEL	*[Hugging him]* Dan, he's gone – he's gone!
EMMA	And Val, do I understand … that deed of gift, we might render it null and void?
VAL	Oh yes. Allcard versus Skinner. I have the print-out here …
EMMA	I'll take your word, if that's OK. So, Mr Loyal, you've heard – well, I guess, too much. We're in your hands.

PAMELA	If he dares –
EMMA	Pamela, please! There's no grand tale of sex here, but my husband's name for probity and sense … ?
DES	Yes, what's my game to be *[sucking his teeth again]* ? "Sacked Tory toff –
PAMELA	Really!
EMMA	Quiet, Pam!
DES	– exposes fraud in heartless time-share scam". Clickbait for the kids at the Shocker Online. Nah! Let's keep it old school – Page One headline for our older readers. No need to complicate their lives with irony. Not with the state, you know, of their attention span. I'll be on my way. Unless the old girl could see her way to give a grandma's view?
PAMELA	Clem, tell your friend I am appointed Dame Commander of the British Empire, but plain Mrs. Ogden will do.
DES	I'll take that as a 'no'. Ta ta, one and all.

He heads for the hall door, then turns back

[To Charles] Tell you what, if you like we can have a shot at restarting your political career. Our readers love a have-a-go hero. "High noon in the suburb, as Tory Grandee lamps conman. Said Charlie Ogden, sixty-three –

CHARLES	Fifty-four!
DES	Older is better. " – seemed time to take the law into my own hands. Vulnerable women entrapped by a love rat – the courts just give 'em a slap. If they want a scrap I'll take 'em on, Dirty Harry style." There you go. That should restore the smile

on your constituent's faces – and the PM.

CHARLES   I'm a bit confused. Remind me, Em,
            do you remember me saying this reprehensible
            guff?

EMMA   No, darling, you're far, far too sensible.

DES   There, dear Em, I have to disagree with you.

CHARLES   The thing is, Des, it simply isn't true.
            From now on, I think, truth will be my guideline.
            But I'll give you a scoop. I'm to resign
            from Parliament altogether.

DES   I beg your pardon.

CHARLES   If you like, I'm going to cultivate my garden.

PAMELA   Stop this, Charles. One inexplicable mistake
            is quite enough, please don't make another. Take
            a moment to reconsider, to reflect.

CHARLES   Sorry, Mother. People should expect
            better from their MP when they've given their votes.
            Let's enjoy the whiff of burning boats.

PAMELA   You can't be serious. The Ogdens' place
            is in the House!

CHARLES   Not anymore. Please face
            that fact.
                                                A silence
PAMELA   Fuck!
                                She picks up her bag and exits
DES   "Sweary granny in Ogden family ruck!"
                                    The front door bangs
            That isn't quite the tale I'd hoped.
            Nor "Time-share hero quitting in remorse" … Nope,
            too multi-layered to give it real fire.
            But, your choice. This way – salute that friendly briar
            rose.

Exit DES via the French window. Those that remain exchange looks

CLEM	Charles, you really ought … a spot of this? You owe it to yourself. A toast to hubris.
CHARLES	[His eyes on Danuta] No, not now.
CLEM	Emma? Mel? Daniel? Val?

CLEM begins to pour Glen Ord. DANUTA makes to exit

| CHARLES | Danuta don't go. |
| DANUTA | No words, no chat, Charlie. Too many words, you English. You make friends again with family. I put dish to cook, to celebrate. |

DANUTA exits

| CHARLES | But – yes, yes, of course. Val – |

But VAL is focused on MELISSA, who won't catch his eye. EMMA steers CHARLES away, then starts to leaf through music. VAL begins to return papers to his bag …

MELISSA	That was amazing, Val. How had you heard … ?
VAL	Danuta called me, fed me that password, and a tip or two on how to steer round any internal firewalls I found.
MELISSA	The indispensable Danuta!

VAL nods. A silence

| CLEM | Charles, in Monday's column do I confute a story of undue influence, or spell out all the gory details? Now that's what I what I call a dilemma! |

VAL turns to leave

| EMMA | I so remember, you two, how well you danced at that December ball we had last year. Is this it, Dan? |
| DANIEL | Oh, yes … |

They start to play a romantic dance tune. After a few moments MEL and VAL come together to dance

| CLEM | Oh, Daniel, by the way you didn't tell us – what's the play? |

CHARLES	What play?
CLEM	He's got a part, Charles. Didn't you hear?
DANIEL	It's 'The Imposter' by Molière. I play the son. He shouts a bit, gets mad in parts –
CLEM	A remarkable reversal of life and art.
DANIEL	– but still a peachy role. Rehearsals start a fortnight from today. And the pay's all right. Well, Equity basic, but that's OK. *And* it's going to be in modern dress.
CLEM	Well, why not? Like this *[his scotch]*, Molière is timeless.

EMMA and DANIEL pick up the tune again, MELISSA and VAL dance
on, but then the lights change and the Ogdens freeze. Enter
TARTUFFE. He is on the phone …

TARTUFFE	… Yeah, in dollars. Heathrow Terminal 3.

Shuts off the phone. Notices the audience

What? Thought you'd seen the last of me?
The trough here's empty, had all I can scoff.
So here's to Old England! Time to bugger off –
no point in stopping – and hello USA!
The set-up over there gets better every day.
You have to watch your back, but if you press
the triggers right, you're guaranteed success.
I'll rake in billions on my start-up loan
from Mum. Thirty K, every cent she owns.

Notices the frozen figures of the Ogdens

Still here are we? What, penny hasn't dropped?
Come on, wake up! You lot have just been cropped
out of the picture. You never saw me coming.
Fun for me, though, a nifty bit of slumming
'mong the elite, and working out the trick.
Selling Tartuffe's legend was a bigger kick
than sex in fact.

DANUTA enters reading a copy of Scientific American. The Ogdens
unfreeze
Oy, you, don't turn your backs
on me, I've not finished with you yet.
So liberal and smug, you just don't get it.
I'm the malware that makes the mainframe crash,
the virus in your inbox primed to trash
all the codes, so don't you dare ignore me.
Oh, fuck off then! You've begun to really bore me.
You had your chance, your sort always blow it.
I'm going now. You're dead. You just don't know it.

He doesn't move. The lights fade to black.

Andrew Hilton is a director, actor and writer. He founded *Shakespeare at the Tobacco Factory* in 1999 and remained its Artistic Director until 2017, directing nearly 40 productions for the company – Shakespeare, Chekhov, Molière, Stoppard and other classics. In his early career he wrote and directed plays for young audiences at London's Mermaid Theatre and wrote for BBC Schools Radio; more recently he has written on Chekhov production for Radio 3 and lectured on Shakespeare. As an actor he has played seasons at the National Theatre and the Bristol Old Vic, toured extensively from New York to Tokyo, and made numerous appearances in film, television and radio. In 2013 he was made an Honorary Doctor of Letters by the University of Bristol for his services to theatre in the city.

Dominic Power writes for the stage, radio and opera. His original works for the theatre include *Gillfins* (Old Red Lion) and *Tales of the Undead* (Bristol's Hen & Chicken & Croydon Warehouse) while his work for BBC Radio has encompassed adaptations, original dramas and short stories. His opera libretti include *Brief Encounter* for the composer Peter Weigold and *The Doll Behind the Curtain* for Amir Mahyar Tafreshipour. From 1999 to 2015  he was Head of Screen Arts at the National Film & Television School. He has worked as Andrew Hilton's associate throughout Shakespeare at the Tobacco Factory's history, providing radical versions of *Measure for Measure, The Changeling, The Taming of the Shrew, The Comedy of Errors, Two Gentlemen of Verona, The School for Scandal* and *All's Well that Ends Well*.